FROM
ADVERSITY
TO
SUCCESS,

WISDOM OF THE GENERALS

AND FROM
FEAR
TO
VICTORY

HOW TO TRIUMPH IN BUSINESS AND IN LIFE

WILLIAM A. COHEN, PH.D.
MAJOR GENERAL, USAFR, RET.

Prentice
Hall Press

Library of Congress Cataloging-in-Publication Data

Cohen, William A.
    Wisdom of the generals. / [compiled] by William A. Cohen.
        p.   cm.
    Includes bibliographical references and index.
    ISBN 0-7352-0167-6
      1. Armed forces—Officers—Quotations. 2. Command of troops—Quotations, maxims,
etc. 3. Strategy—Quotations, maxims, etc. 4. Leadership—Quotations, maxims, etc.
5. Quotations, English. I. Title.

UB210.C64 2001
355.3'3041—dc21   00-038551
                                                  CIP

Acquisitions Editor: *Tom Power*
Production Editor: *Jacqueline Roulette*
Formatting/Interior Design: *Robyn Beckerman*

Printed in the United States of America

10 9 8 7 6 5 4 3 2 1

ISBN 0-7352-0167-6

 Paramus, NJ 07652

http://www.phdirect.com

CONTENTS

PART III
THE AFTER ACTION REPORT
The Contributors and What They Did / 167

INDEX / 227

PART I

BEFORE THE BATTLE:

Introduction

"Praise the Lord and pass the ammunition."

—Chaplain Howell M. Forgy
of the cruiser USS New Orleans in
battle during the Japanese
attack at Pearl Harbor,
December 7th, 1941

WHY APPLY WISDOM FROM WAR TO CIVILIAN PURSUITS?

Are battle insights a successful model for advice in succeeding in our business and personal lives? What a strange and awful notion. What does battle success have to do with success in business, romance, finding a job, or raising kids? Many would reject such a concept out of hand with a straightforward and uncompromising argument. War is absolutely undesirable and repulsive. It is waged ruthlessly and causes untold human misery. Moreover, no cause is worth dying for. War is therefore without any redeeming qualities. To suggest any aspect of warfare as a model for other human endeavors is an abomination.

Many who use battle as a model for success in other competitive activities do so with a basic assumption that translates roughly into "business is war." That is, competition in any activity promoted as analogous to warfare is so extreme that it should be viewed as extreme as warfare itself.

Interestingly many former soldiers reject this argument. They point out that no business campaign requires competitors to routinely risk their lives to win or to operate in such a violent environment. However, it is important to recognize what is being rejected. It is not ideas or concepts learned in war to be applied elsewhere. It is accepting these concepts whole cloth because the activity and warfare are said to be identical in their demands which is clearly untrue.

Most professional soldiers would agree that war is terrible and undesirable. In fact, soldiers would probably be the first to agree with its undesirability, because when it occurs, they are the ones that must fight and suffer. Most, however, would reject the idea that there is no cause worth fighting or dying for. To state that freedom is worth fighting and dying for sounds almost banal. Yet most would agree that it most certainly is. Similarly, there are some causes that are so inherently evil, that not to fight against them is far more terrible and undesirable than warfare.

However, even if we accept that rejecting everything about war is throwing the baby out with the bath water, what is so attractive about this particular baby? That is, what good can come of what is considered horrible by both practitioners and outside observers alike?

War is the most prevalent of all human activities. Someone once calculated that in the entire recorded history of human life on this planet going back some 7000 years, we have been without significant fighting somewhere for less than 100 days. Enormous human effort, thinking, and resources have been concentrated on solving the challenge of winning in battle. More wealth has been expended on wars than on any other endeavor. Our earliest recorded writings are about warfare. Many of the greatest thinkers have been concerned with it, and one only needs to look at the Bible to note that this is no less true of our religious writers. My point is, with all this expenditure of time, resources, energy, and cost in human life, we must have learned some lessons that are universally true and applicable. Further, these lessons could not have resulted from other fields if for no other reason than because the investment in these other fields has been so miniscule in comparison.

However, there are other reasons. In an introduction to an earlier book on leadership, I pointed out, "Battle leadership probably represents the greatest leadership challenge for any leader. In combat, conditions are severe. There are terrible hazards. There are poor 'working conditions.' There is probably greater uncertainty than in any other type of human activity . . . 'Workers' may need to perform their duties with little food and irregular sleep. All must take great risks. Most followers and leaders alike would prefer to be somewhere else and doing something else. While there are true military geniuses in battle, the vast majority, as in most organizations, are ordinary men and women.

In most battles, many are not professionals. Not all are suited to their jobs. Professional or amateur, all are stressed far more than in any civilian situation or occupation. Moreover, leaders must not only carry out the mission, but do their best to protect the lives of those they lead at the same time. So, battle probably represents a 'worst case' condition. No wonder traditional motivators such as high pay, good benefits, and job security aren't much good. There is no 'business as usual' on the battlefield.[1]

But I was not the first to note that concepts from battle were applicable to other situations. One of the foremost military strategists of the twentieth century was Britisher B.H. Liddell Hart. In his analysis of hundreds of campaigns, Liddell Hart discovered what he called the "indirect approach." Liddell Hart found that you were far more likely to achieve success in battle by attacking your objective in an indirect fashion than meeting it head-on.

"When in the course of studying a long series of military campaigns, I first came to perceive the superiority of the indirect over the direct approach, I was looking merely for light upon strategy. With deepened reflection, however, I began to realize that the indirect approach had a much wider application—that it was a law of life in all spheres: a truth of philosophy. Its fulfillment was seen to be the key to practical achievement in dealing with any problem where the human factor predominates, and a conflict of wills tends to spring from an underlying concern for interests. In all such cases, the direct assault of new ideas provokes a stubborn resistance, thus intensifying the difficulty of producing a change in outlook. Conversion is achieved more easily and rapidly by unsuspected infiltration of a different idea or by an argument that turns the flank of instinctive opposition. The indirect approach is as fundamental to the realm of politics as to the realm of

---

[1] William A. Cohen, *The Stuff of Heroes: The Eight Universal Laws of Leadership* (Marietta, Georgia: Longstreet Press, 1998) p 1–2.

sex. In commerce, the suggestion that there is a bargain to be secured is far more potent than any direct appeal to buy. And in any sphere it is proverbial that the surest way of gaining a superior's acceptance of a new idea is to persuade him that it is his idea! As in war, the aim is to weaken resistance before attempting to overcome it; and the effect is best attained by drawing the other party out of his defenses."[2]

In the field of management Peter F. Drucker, arguably the number one management thinker of our time, claims that the first systematic book on leadership, written by Xenophon 2000 years ago, is still the best. Xenophon was a general who is also quoted in this book, and his book was on combat leadership. Similarly, Philip Kotler is considered by many to be the leading marketing theorist in business. Kotler has taken various offensive and defensive military maneuvers and applied them directly to marketing activities, even retaining their original military designations.

Wisdom of the Generals offers more than 300 contributions from more than one hundred generals and admirals going all the way back to the earliest days of recorded history. I have categorized this great body of wisdom into more than sixty topic categories from adversity to vision and illustrated the application of what these great minds have said about warfare to other activities. In reality, I have barely scratched the surface regarding the potential of what is offered. A little reflection on applying the advice of these masters to whatever question is under consideration can yield tremendous assistance and insight to any issue.

---

[2]B.H. Liddell Hart, *Strategy, Revised Ed.* (New York: Frederick A Prager, 1961) p. 18.

PART II

THE BATTLE:

THE WISDOM OF THE GENERALS AND ADMIRALS

"Hear counsel, and receive instruction, that you may be wise in the days to come."

—Proverbs 19:20

ADVERSITY

Campaigns and battles are nothing but a long series of difficulties to be overcome. The lack of equipment, the lack of food, the lack of this or that; the real leader displays his quality in his triumphs over adversity, however great it may be.

GENERAL OF THE ARMY GEORGE C. MARSHALL, U.S. Army

I'm a hell of a general when I'm winning, anybody is, but it's when you're not winning—and I have not always been winning . . . —it is then that the real test of leadership is made.

FIELD MARSHAL SIR WILLIAM SLIM, British Army

It is the property of ordinary men, in times of danger, to see difficulties more clearly than advantages, and to shrink from steps which involve risk.

REAR ADMIRAL ALFRED THAYER MAHAN, U.S. Navy

"Difficulties" is the name given to things which it is our business to overcome.

ADMIRAL OF THE FLEET ERNEST J. KING, U.S. Navy

How many things apparently impossible have nevertheless been performed by resolute men who had no alternative but death!

NAPOLEON BONAPARTE, French Emperor

What could be more difficult than accomplishing a task in the challenging environment of the battlefield? Yet, those who are in this environment rarely have an alternative. To be successful, they must overcome great difficulties. As General Marshall points out, these difficulties are manifold and may include lack of food, lack of equipment, insufficient resources of every type including both material and manpower . . . even lack of sleep! Moreover, these problems probably are not short-lived, but may persist throughout a campaign lasting months. Under these circumstances, the real leader keeps going despite the adversity.

Mary Kay Ash, Chairperson Emeritus of Mary Kay Cosmetics, the woman who became famous by giving pink Cadillacs to her most successful salespeople, says that the successful salesperson and the successful leader must learn to take lemons (problems) and turn them into lemonade (opportunities). She did it herself when a few short weeks before she was to open her business, her husband died of a heart attack, taking away what was to have been her source of income and support while building her business. She already had invested her life savings of $5,000. So, she made lemonade, determined that instead of becoming profitable after a year, she would need to become profitable almost immediately. And she did it, building a billion-dollar corporation and giving tens of thousands of women the opportunity to earn high income at a time when most could not. As Napoleon points out, how many impossible things become possible if men (or women) are determined to overcome adversity and make it so?

Sure, it's easy to succeed when you have no adversity to overcome, but this is often not the case in life. Field Marshal Slim notes that he was considered one heck of a smart operator when he was successful. The problem was, he had failures, too. Everyone does, and everyone has problems. As someone said, there are no dreams without dragons. It is slaying those dragons and overcoming your adversities that are the real tests that you face whether you are on the battlefield or selling Mary Kay Cosmetics. And then, how sweet is the victory!

Unfortunately, many see only the dragons, and simply give up. What a tragedy! How terrible it would have beeen for Mary Kay if she had only focused on the unfortunate sudden death of her husband and the lack of income she had counted on. What would have happened had she given up? Many others would have. How terrible it would have been for the tens of thousands of women who have profited from the opportunity she created for them, and the millions of customers who swear by her products. Admiral Mahan finds that ordinary people simply see the downside too clearly, and so they shrink from the task and quit because of adversity they consider overwhelming. Yet, Admiral King says that difficulties are simply the name of things it is our business to overcome.

Years ago, when I was a first-year cadet at West Point, we were told that the only acceptable responses to an upper classman's inquiry were "yes sir!," "no sir!" and "no excuse sir!" It was difficult at first. Our prior experiences at home and at school had taught us to respond to criticism by immediately making excuses. Now we were being taught that there was no excuse, regardless of the difficulties and adversities that we faced. And believe me, there were plenty.

Now you may think that's a little extreme. After all, there are sometimes real reasons, physical laws of man or nature which cannot be overcome. No excuse, sir, indeed! But I want to tell you something. That extreme attitude and being corrected for infractions that were our responsibility taught me a lesson in accountability which has lasted a lifetime. Before, I thought adversity meant that there was always an excuse. Afterwards, I thought the opposite. I think that there must always be a way of overcoming adversity or the difficulties of any situation if I just look hard enough. And guess what? In most cases I have found this to be true.

Many successful people I have met and talked with, both in and out of the military, have come to the same conclusion. They feel there is always a way. Successful people do what unsuccessful people simply won't do. I have modified this in leadership to reflect that successful leaders do what less successful leaders simply won't do. In truth, this is true of all human actions or endeavors. Successful men and women face the same degree of adversity as others do. But they believe there is always a way to overcome it.

About adversity, the wisdom of the generals is:

* All successful projects are simply a long series of adversities which must be overcome.

* Far from it being unusual to face adversity, it is normal, and it is our business to overcome it.

* The real test is not when we are successful when there is no adversity, but when there is and we triumph.

* When we face these challenges and position them so that we feel we have no alternative, that there can be no excuses, we can accomplish the impossible.

AGGRESSIVENESS

It is even better to act quickly and err than to hesitate until the time of action is past.
                                    MAJOR GENERAL CARL VON CLAUSEWITZ, Prussian Army

Action is the governing rule of war.
                                    FIELD MARSHAL FERDINAND FOCH, French Army

Our Country will, I believe, sooner forgive an officer for attacking an enemy than for letting it alone.
                                    ADMIRAL LORD HORATIO NELSON, Royal Navy

I do not advise rashness, but I do desire resolute and actual fighting, with necessary casualties.
                                    GENERAL PHILIP H. SHERIDAN, U.S. Army

Find out where your enemy is. Get at him as soon as you can and as often as you can, and keep moving on.
                                    GENERAL ULYSSES S. GRANT, U.S. Army

To some, the word "aggressiveness" sounds negative. Maybe we think of a fast-talking salesman who tries to persuade us to buy something. Or, maybe our thoughts turn to an obnoxious individual we know who always seems to be trying to intimidate others.

The military uses this term in quite a different way. It means someone who is proactive in approaching any task or assignment. This person never hesitates, but actively pursues a positive result in any situation until he or she is successful. This person must not hesitate, for as General von Clausewitz says, it is better to err than to wait to take action until it is too late.

Too often, we put off making a decision until the decision is made for us. Instead of taking charge ourselves, we put ourselves in the hands of fate. Why do we do this? Frequently it is because we are afraid of making a mistake. Yet, delaying is worse, because when we surrender to fate, fate rarely gives us the outcome we would prefer. So, Clausewitz tells us it is always better to plunge in. And Field Marshal Foch agrees, telling us that it is action that governs war. But in truth, it is action that governs all of our affairs in life.

How many great ideas have you had that you put off suggesting or implementing until "just the right time?" But just the right time never came, and one day you were frustrated to see that someone else had taken "your" idea and introduced it into the marketplace.

No one appropriated your idea. Your problem was a lack of aggressiveness in this instance. Lord Nelson, England's great sea admiral during the Napoleonic wars well knew that it was far better to attack an enemy (aggressively pursue an opportunity) than simply to ignore it because of the threat of potential costs or because you had incomplete information.

Once I wrote a book called *Making It* (Prentice Hall, 1993) with entrepreneur E. Joseph Cossman. Joe Cossman had made a fortune with products ranging from his "ant farm" to a solid insect poison. He sold millions of his products and made millions of dollars along the way. Yet Joe entered business not only without the benefit of an MBA, but without any college at all. He plunged right in, not hesitating, but learning all he could along the way.

Of course Joe would have preferred to have had a good business education before he started . . . and he actually got an MBA later on in life. But Joe didn't let anything stand in the way of what he wanted to do. He made lots of mistakes, but he also became a millionaire many times over. I don't know if Joe ever knew what General Sheridan said about campaigning during the Civil War. He didn't advise rashness, but he sure as heck knew that you couldn't win battles without fighting. And yes, unfortunately there would be casualties along the way.

Sheridan had been trained as an infantry officer. And all his prior service had been in that branch. But that didn't stop him from becoming Grant's overall cavalry commander. President Abraham Lincoln told "Little Phil" Sheridan that previous to his meeting him, that he thought a cavalry commander had to be over six feet tall, but now he understood that five feet four inches would do just fine. Sheridan may not have fit the cavalry mode perfectly in experience or physical appearance, but who cared? He was successful anyway. He was aggressive and after due consideration, he plunged in.

It is his commander, General Grant, that tells us that the key is simple. It is to find the enemy and get at him, and keep getting at him. In a universal sense he wasn't talking about the enemy so much as he was speaking of any opportunity. You have to find the opportunity, go after it, and keep going after it until you have it. This holds for a teenager interested in someone he or she meets as a candidate for the big dance. It holds for anyone wanting to start a business. It holds for an investor seeking an opportunity to create wealth.

That's why aggressiveness is not such a bad thing. If we adopt the concept, it will help us reach any goal or objective we choose.

About aggressiveness, the wisdom of the generals is:

* Don't hesitate, take action.
* Don't worry about potential mistakes, you'll make them anyway—press on!
* The key is to find the opportunity, and then to pursue it and keep pursuing it until you attain the desired result.

ATTITUDE

In war, moral considerations make up three-quarters of the game; the relative balance of manpower accounts only for the remaining quarter.

NAPOLEON BONAPARTE, Emperor of France

Do not compare your physical forces with those of the enemy's, for the spirit should not be compared with matter.

GENERAL SIMÓN BOLÍVAR, South American Revolutionary

It is the cold glitter in the attacker's eye not the point of the questing bayonet that breaks the line.

GENERAL GEORGE S. PATTON, JR., U.S. Army

It is your attitude, and the suspicion that you are maturing the boldest designs against him, that imposes on your enemy.

FREDERICK THE GREAT, German Emperor

What counts is not the size of the dog in the fight, but the size of fight in the dog.

GENERAL OF THE ARMY DWIGHT D. EISENHOWER, U.S. Army

People with the right attitude are almost impossible to beat. That's because it counts for a lot more than you might imagine. Napoleon says three-quarters of the game is attitude. Do you think that this is an overstatement?

I consult for, and I am on the Academic Advisory Board of a company called Vector Marketing, Inc. Vector Marketing is well over $100 million in sales, but they sell primarily one class of product: high quality cutlery under the brand name "Cutco." These are mostly kitchen knives, but one of their divisions, K-bar, made the original and world-famous Marine Corps k-bar knife during World War II.

Vector is especially interested in working with academics, because most of their sales force are students working part time and virtually all of Vector's management, right on up through company president were once salespeople.

I was a strong supporter of Vector long before I became a consultant to them because of what they teach my students: goal setting, time management, entrepreneurship, leadership . . . the list goes on and on. But perhaps most important of all is the winning attitude they impart.

Let me give you an example. Two years ago, a young student by the name of Zach Lutsky had to put himself through college. He became a very successful Vector salesperson. He didn't have much choice, as his tuition was expensive. Zach wanted to go to medical school after graduation. Unfortunately hard work and good grades do not always go together. His counselor told him that there was no way he could get into medical school. On the face of it, there was not. Zach didn't have the grades. Nor did he fall into some category of special admissions. But he did have the strong positive attitude and faith in himself he developed as a Vector salesperson. On being rejected by the medical school of his choice, he called the dean of the school asking if he could fly out for a face-to-face interview. The dean reluctantly granted the interview, stating there was no way he would be able to enter medical school with his grades . . . there were just so many openings, and it was just too competitive. Zach convinced the dean to meet with him anyway.

At the interview, Zach explained how he had had to work to put himself through college. He showed the dean his track record as a salesperson. He made the point that the success he had achieved selling cutlery had taught him lessons which were directly transferable to the ability to succeed, both in medical school and afterwards. The dean was impressed and told him so. But, there were no openings. The dean advised him to prepare himself further and to apply again the following year, although he still could hold out little hope.

Zach returned to his home town in Thousand Oaks, California and made plans to follow the dean's advice. He was going to try again the following year. However, three days before medical school was to start, he received a telegram from the dean's office. There had been a last minute cancellation of someone who had already been admitted. Zach was told to be there in three days. Because of Zach's indomitable attitude, he did the impossible and entered medical school with less than "competitive grades." And his first year grades in medical school? Straight A's.

Simón Bolívar says don't bother comparing the physical with the spiritual, you just can't do it. Patton advises us to look not at the bayonet, but the "glitter in the eye." I guess that's what the dean did when he made the decision to admit this young man to medical school despite his grades.

What about our competitors? Are they affected by our attitude? You bet they are. I've been on enough boards and worked with enough companies to state unequivocally that the mere presence of certain executives in a competitor's camp is enough to cause sleepless nights and the diversion of millions of dollars in resources.

Eisenhower lays it out for us clearly. What he is saying is that it doesn't make any difference what resources we have or lack. Our attitude counts more: three to one if we agree with the Emperor Napoleon.

About attitude, the wisdom of the generals tell us:

* Attitude is more important even than physical facts.

* Don't worry too much about what you have or have not on your side; it's the desire inside you that counts.

* If you really want something, go for it—don't be deterred by anything or anyone that says you can't.

AUDACITY

In war, nothing is impossible, providing you use audacity.

GENERAL GEORGE S. PATTON, JR., U.S. Army

In audacity and obstinacy will be found safety.

NAPOLEON BONAPARTE, French Emperor

A bold vigorous assault has won many a faltering cause.

GENERAL IRA C. EAKER, U.S. Air Force

Damn the torpedoes! Full speed ahead!

ADMIRAL DAVID G. FARRAGUT, U.S. Navy

When the situation is obscure, attack.

COLONEL GENERAL HEINZ GUDERIAN, German Army

The dictionary tells us that audacity means to be daring and bold. Be bold, General Patton tells us, and you can accomplish the impossible. If the situation is in doubt or unclear, be bold says World War II German Panzer Leader General Heinz Guderian. A bold, vigorous assault carries even a faltering cause agrees General Ira Eaker, who once commanded the mighty 8th Air Force in assaults against Hitler's "Fortress Europe." Does your operation face great risk or adversity? Act with boldness. Therein lies safety, Napoleon tells us.

W. Clement Stone had his own insurance agency in Chicago. He had acquired the right to sell insurance for one of the largest companies in America and was doing pretty well at it. The trouble was, his agents were doing a little too well. They were taking business away from the in-house agents of one of the largest companies for which Stone's agency was selling.

While on vacation he suddenly learned that this company would terminate his contract to sell their insurance within a couple of days.

Unfortunately, this represented most of his business. Many of his employees felt that the only alternative was bankruptcy. They anticipated looking for new jobs. Instead, Stone met with the president of this company and convinced him to give him a few weeks of additional time before having to cease selling his insurance. In that time, Stone acted with great boldness and formed his own insurance company. Recently, his company, the AON Corporation, reached $6 billion in annual sales with 27,000 employees.

Union Admiral Farragut was in command at the Battle of Mobile Bay on August 5th, 1864. His fleet consisted of four ironclad monitors and fourteen wooden ships. He had himself lashed to the rigging of his flagship *U.S.S. Hartford.* As he crossed under the deadly Confederate gunfire of Mobile's harbor defenses, a mine blew up his leading monitor, the *U.S.S. Tecumseh.* This stopped his fleet's advance. Some officers suggested an immediate retreat. Farragut didn't agree. Turning the *Hartford* into the minefield to clear the way, he gave the famous command, "Damn the Torpedoes! Full speed ahead!" The other mines failed to go off, and Farragut entered Mobile Bay victoriously.

Farragut's lesson to us echoes down through the years. How many times do we find ourselves stopped after having exploded a mine causing serious damage while on the way to reach an objective? Sure, sometimes this tells us we should seek another way. However, this is not always true. There is no certainty that we will hit other mines, or if we do whether they will explode, or even whether there are any other mines. Sometimes it's best simply to give the command, "Damn the Torpedoes! Full speed ahead!" and proceed.

When the Germans shocked the allies with a surprise offensive during the closing days of World War II in the winter of 1944–45, many were in panic. Senior commanders considered how far to retreat before the allied lines could be re-established and defended against the Germans. Only Patton talked not about retreat, but attack. He convinced his colleagues, and got authority to pivot the line of advance of his weary troops ninety degrees and to go on the offensive and attack boldly into the flank of the Germans. Patton's audacity turned a defeat into an even greater victory which shortened the war.

The wisdom of the generals says this about audacity:

* When the situation is unclear, act boldly.

* When the situation is in doubt, act boldly—security lies in boldness.

* When there are obstacles, act boldly.

* If you would do the impossible . . . you must act boldly!

CARING

Only after the men are settled in their encampment does the general retire; only after all the cooks have finished their cooking does he go in and eat . . .

T'AI KUNG CHIANG SHANG, Ancient Chinese General

If you wish to be loved by your soldiers, do not lead them to slaughter.

FREDERICK THE GREAT, German Emperor

A reflective reading of history will show that no man ever rose to military greatness who could not convince his troops that he put them first, above all else.

GENERAL MAXWELL D. TAYLOR, U.S. Army

For people are only too glad to obey the man who they believe takes wiser thoughts for their interests than they themselves do.

XENOPHON, Ancient Greek General

Place the care and protection of the men first; share their hardships without complaint and when the real test comes you will find that they possess a genuine respect and admiration for you.

GENERAL ALEXANDER M. PATCH, U.S. Army

D own through the ages, military leaders give us a consistent lesson in caring. Caring is about caring for those that report to you and for whom you are therefore responsible. It is about caring for your customers. It is about caring for others more than you care for yourself.

From ancient generals like Xenophon and T'ai Kung Chiang Shang right on up through modern times, they all say the same thing. If you want to be a real leader, you must always put the interests of those who report to you ahead of your own personal interests.

I am painfully aware that leaders in many organizations don't demonstrate this level of caring. They do not share hardships, as General Patch advises. Rather than eat after all others have done so, as T'ai Kung Chiang Shang requires, they eat first or sleep first, or take other advantages of their position which demonstrates a lack of, rather than a predisposition towards, caring for those who work for them. Are you one who reports to such a leader? Well, how do you feel about his or her actions? Are you motivated by that leader's lack of caring to do great things for your organization? I rather doubt it.

The same goes for unofficial leaders, that is, individuals who hold no official position in the company, yet are leaders nonetheless. One of the reasons these "uncrowned" leaders are able to get others to follow them is that they demonstrate a level of caring for others . . . so in return, others care for and are ready to follow them as well.

Before taking advantage of others whom you want to motivate, you'd first better think a little about the results of General Maxwell Taylor's reading and reflection. It is that no man ever rose to military greatness who could not convince his troops that he put them first, above all else.

But is it really above all else? Well, no. There is also the mission of the organization. Sometimes the mission must come first, before those wonderful people you care for. That's okay, so long as the mission comes before you do, and it isn't really the mission that is motivating you just so you can further your own career. Then, you should think about Frederick the Great's admonition: if you want to be loved (and respected) you certainly better not lead your people to slaughter, or failure or the loss of their jobs. Part of this has to do with competence, something we will have more to say about later. But the greater part is not to sacrifice them for stupid reasons. This is a corruption of putting the mission first, and certainly violates any pretence at caring.

About caring, the wisdom of the generals is:

★ Always take care of your people in every way.

★ Put the interests of those who report to you and your customers' interests before your own.

★ Yes, the mission comes first, but not as an adjunct of your interests or to enhance your own career.

CHANGE

You are told by commencement speakers that you have got to go out and change the world. Well, you've got only one year to do it. Next year, another corps of graduates will be told the same thing.

ADMIRAL HYMAN RICKOVER, U.S. Navy

They will probably persist in their errors for some time, and submit to be repeatedly defeated, before they will be reconciled to such a change—so reluctant are all nations to relinquish old customs.

FIELD MARSHAL MAURICE COMTE DE SAXE, French Army

A tramp cannot tolerate a bath, and the average general cannot tolerate any change in pre-conceived ideas; prejudice sticks to his brain like tar to a blanket.

MAJOR GENERAL J.F.C. FULLER, British Army

No rule of war is so absolute as to allow no exceptions.

NAPOLEON BONAPARTE, French Emperor

The principles of yesterday no longer apply . . . We must think in terms of tomorrow. We must bear in mind that air power itself can become obsolete.

GENERAL OF THE AIR FORCE HENRY H. ARNOLD, U.S. Air Force

There's no doubt about it. More than anything else, we fear change. This is human nature. There is a certain comfort in doing things the way they have always been done; in maintaining the continuity of the past even if the old ways are wrong. Peter F. Drucker, my professor, friend, and probably the greatest management thinker of our time, has said that any organization, no matter how successful, that continues to do what has made it successful in the past, will eventually fail.

What an indictment! This says that every organization must change or fail. Why is this so? Because our environment is one of constant change. The technology of today is not what it was yesterday. Our behavior, our thoughts, our beliefs all change over time. Recently I watched a documentary on smoking. It pointed out that in the 1940's much of the medical community thought that there was no harm in smoking. On film a doctor laughed at those thinking smoking was harmful. "Smoking cigarettes is no more harmful than eating tomatoes," he said. The swimming suits, both male and female, of today would have gotten their wearers arrested for indecent exposure in the time of our grandparents. Competitors, who did not exist previously, suddenly come out of the woodwork. Once we had the field to ourselves. This is no longer true. So change in the environment is inevitable. And we must adapt to this change or fail.

The generals recognize this. No rule is so absolute as to not permit exceptions (a change) states Napoleon. Admiral Rickover, frequently expressing his beliefs in a cynical way tells the new graduates . . . sure, go out and change the world, but don't think your changes are final, or even long term, because next year they'll tell the new graduates the same thing.

Does this mean that all change is good? Of course not. You cannot simply change for the sake of change and expect good things to happen. Likely as not, you will get the opposite effect. I have seen advertisers who drop successful ads simply because they get tired of them, and no other reason. Usually, their profits drop. But, we must not be afraid of change, and should always be open to new ideas.

I think General Arnold's quote is probably the most courageous of those I have included. He and his generation of airmen had fought long and hard to see air power appreciated by the other military services. In this fight, many had their careers terminated for their unconventional views. Finally, the U.S. Army Air Force was separated from the Army and became the independent U.S. Air Force in 1949. Arnold, who had already retired was elevated to the rank of

General of the Air Force (five stars), the first and only one the Air Force has had. Yet, this same individual tells us, "We must think in terms of tomorrow. We must bear in mind that air power itself can become obsolete."

The wisdom of the generals on change is:

* ⋆ Organizations, all organizations, will fight change with all their might, even to the point of accepting failure.

* ⋆ There is no rule of management, marketing, leadership, or life which is absolute.

* ⋆ Never fear change, it is inevitable and can lead to better things.

* ⋆ If we do not accept and encourage change, we will eventually fail.

CHARACTER

If, to please the people, we offer what we ourselves disapprove, how can we afterward defend our work? Let us raise a standard to which the wise and honest can repair.

GENERAL GEORGE WASHINGTON, Continental Army

The union of wise theory with great character will constitute the great captain.

GENERAL HENRI DE JOMINI, French Army, Russian Army

Not only the future of our arms but the well-being of our people depend upon a constant reaffirmation and strengthening of public faith in the virtue and trustworthiness of the officer body . . . By the same reasoning, high character in the military office is a safeguard of the character of the Nation. Anything less than exemplary conduct is therefore unworthy of the commission.

BRIGADIER GENERAL S.L.A. MARSHALL, US Army

Character is the bedrock on which the whole edifice of leadership rests. It is the prime element for which every profession, every corporation, every industry searches in evaluating a member of its organization. With it, the full worth of an individual can be developed. Without it, particularly in the military profession—failure in peace, disaster in war, or, at best mediocrity in both will result.

GENERAL MATHEW B. RIDGWAY, U.S. Army

By greatness of character a general gains command over himself, and by goodness of character he gains command over his men, and those two moods of command express the moral side of generalship.

MAJOR GENERAL J.F.C. FULLER, British Army

It is important for us to recognize what the generals are talking about when they speak of character. They are talking about moral excellence, a high standard of righteous behavior which cannot be denied.

George Washington, speaking about one of the fundamental aspects of character asks how we can defend ourselves if we don't follow our beliefs. Sometimes we cannot do what we would do if we were in authority. We disagree with a decision that was made or is about to be made by someone in authority over us. Then, we are obligated to state our opinion and the reasons for it, no matter how unpopular our opinion, or at variance with our boss's belief. If our boss decides to take the action anyway, we must support it to the best of our ability, or if unable to do so because we consider it an issue of right and wrong rather than just opinion, leave our boss's employ as soon as we can.

Jomini, who wrote one of the classical books on warfare says that it is theory (ability) combined with great character which are the necessary ingredients to make the great captain. This is as true for the great captains of industry, or great political or religious leaders, or leaders in any profession. British General Fuller says this constitutes the moral side of generalship by which we gain command over ourselves and those who report to us.

General Marshall implies that the leader's character is critical for the future of the nation. We can read that to be any organization. Certainly, without character, those that we would have believe in us, in our system, and in our decision-making may fail to do so. General Ridgway goes further and calls character the bedrock of leadership. Without it, he predicts that the organization will ultimately fail, or be mediocre at best. So character, that moral excellence, is of no small importance.

This then, is the wisdom of the generals on character:

* ⋆ Character means having the courage of our beliefs to do and say what is right, and not what is wrong.

* ⋆ Character combined with ability make the "great captain" in any profession.

* ⋆ Through character, we gain control over ourselves and influence over others.

* ⋆ Character is the bedrock of leadership and critical to the future of any organization.

COHESION

Great achievements in war and peace can only result if officers and men form an indissoluble band of brothers.

FIELD MARSHAL PAUL VON HINDENBURG, German Army

My first wish would be that my military family, and the whole Army, should consider themselves as a band of brothers, willing and ready to die for each other.

GENERAL GEORGE WASHINGTON, Continental army

Men who have been in battle know from firsthand experience that when the chips are down, a man fights to help the man next to him . . .

BRIGADIER GENERAL S.L.A. MARSHALL, U.S. Army

Comradeship makes a man feel warm and courageous when all his instincts tend to make him cold and afraid.

FIELD MARSHAL BERNARD MONTGOMERY, British Army

If we start out with the notion of responsibility we find that "comradeship" means "one of all," for each man bears, in his own way and in his own place, a share of the responsibility for the welfare, the ability, the achievements, and the life of others.

COLONEL GENERAL HANS VON SEECKT, German Army

Cohesion means sticking together. It is hard to underrate it. S.L.A. Marshall was a military historian who developed a unique way of doing historical research. He went to the front lines and interviewed everyone from private soldiers to their sergeants and officers, right after the action. He frequently came under fire in doing his research. Afterwards, he analyzed his results.

One of the most amazing things he discovered was that when it was a life or death situation in battle, soldiers soon forgot about their idealism or patriotic reasons for fighting. If things were tough enough, even unit pride lost much of its power. But there was one emotion which never slipped. It was such a strong motivator that soldiers would frequently give up their lives because of it. What was this great motivator? It was not to let their buddies down. Everything else might vanish under the stresses and strains of combat, but not this one feeling. That feeling made all the difference in sticking together, in cohesion.

No wonder that the idea of an army constituting a "band of brothers" should be shared by both 18th century American founding father George Washington and 20th century German Field Marshal von Hindenburg. Our other contributors go on to explain that there is a warmth in being part of this band which comforts and helps when the environment is hostile and that this comradeship means that each individual is one of the whole, bearing part of the responsibility for either success or failure.

It is the wise leader that fosters cohesion for with it, any organization is many times stronger than an organization that lacks it.

Cohesion, according to the wisdom of the generals:

* Is one of the most important elements of organizational productivity.

* Means that every member of the organization bears a responsibility for success or failure.

* Helps motivate members to put the organization's needs above their individual needs.

* Will help the organization attain great achievements.

COMMITMENT

It is fatal to enter any war without the will to win it.

GENERAL OF THE ARMY DOUGLAS MACARTHUR, U.S. Army

If you start to take Vienna—take Vienna.

NAPOLEON BONAPARTE, French Emperor

The merit of the action lies in finishing it to the end.

GENGHIS KHAN, Mongol Ruler

I propose to fight it out on this line, if it takes all summer.

GENERAL ULYSSES S. GRANT, U.S. Army

We will either find a way or make one.

HANNIBAL, Carthaginian General

What the generals are saying here, is that if you are going to do something, then do it. Half-hearted efforts are a total waste of time and resources. Moreover, if you are leading the effort, you can't expect any of your followers to be more committed than you are. So, if you give a nice pep talk about how important some task is, and then leave the scene for more comfortable surroundings, you can expect very little commitment from anyone on this "important" task.

If the task is truly crucial (General MacArthur talks about a war) you simply shouldn't get involved unless you plan to go all the way. In business, it's just plain stupid and perhaps unfair to those who follow you. In war, it's criminal.

Lincoln instantly grasped the difference between Ulysses S. Grant and many of his other generals. "I cannot spare this man," Lincoln said. "He fights." When someone pointed out rumors that Grant drank, Lincoln retorted, "Tell me his brand so that I may send the same to all my generals." William T. Sherman, who succeeded Grant as General-in-Chief after the Civil War and Grant had been elected President said, "I know more about strategy, logistics, and every aspect of military employment than he. However, there is one aspect in which Grant beats me and everyone else. He runs into problems and it doesn't bother him. He keeps pressing on. Those same problems scare the hell out of me and would cause me to hesitate."

After Grant had been promoted to General-in-Chief by Lincoln, Lee asked his most trusted deputy, Lieutenant General James "Pete" Longstreet about him. Longstreet had known Grant at West Point and had been one of his best friends. In fact, Longstreet had served as Grant's best man when he was married. "Tell me about this new fellow," Lee asked. "You knew him well, and to tell the truth, I cannot even remember what he looks like from the Mexican War." Longstreet's answer was to the effect of "Boss, we've got big troubles." Longstreet knew that Grant simply wouldn't quit.

Genghis Khan may not have been educated at West Point, Sandhurst, St. Cyr, or any other military academy, but he clearly understood the essence and importance of commitment. He cuts right to the chase when he tells us that the benefit of any action lies in completing it. How many good and worthy projects have you started that you never completed?

Hannibal led elephants from Africa across the Alps and into ancient Rome to get at his opponents. The Romans said it couldn't be done. Weren't they surprised! Later, at the Battle of Cannae, Hannibal took on 70,000 determined, well-trained, well-fed Romans with about one-quarter of that number of his Carthaginians. In the most decisive battle in the history of warfare, he not only won; he left 80% of the Romans dead on the battlefield. "We will find a way, or make one," he said.

According to the wisdom of the generals:

* ★ If you are going to start something, finish it; otherwise don't start it.
* ★ No matter how tough things are, or how long they may take . . . fight it out "if it takes all summer."
* ★ If you can't find a way, make one.
* ★ The merit of any action is in completing it.

COMPETENCE

Officers can never act with competence until they are masters of their profession.

MAJOR GENERAL HENRY KNOX, Continental Army

I think the military and civil talents are distinct if not different, and full duty in either sphere is about as much as one man can qualify himself to perform . . . We should have neither military statesmen nor political generals.

GENERAL ROBERT E. LEE, Confederate States Army

A competent leader can get efficient service from poor troops, while on the contrary an incapable leader can demoralize the best of troops.

GENERAL OF THE ARMIES JOHN J. PERSHING, U.S. ARMY

I believe I owe most of my success to the attention I always paid to the inferior part of tactics as a regimental officer.

FIELD MARSHAL ARTHUR WELLESLEY, The Duke of Wellington, British Army

The American soldier expects his sergeant to be able to teach him how to do his job. And he expects even more from his officers.

GENERAL OF THE ARMY OMAR N. BRADLEY, U.S. Army

You read a lot about the importance of office politics to get ahead. And if this weren't enough, in our elementary schools some years ago, someone got the bright idea that it was discouraging to fail anyone. They came up with the idea of "social promotions." So we started passing students on to the next grade not based on competence or knowing anything, but simply based on being there. That was supposed to give these students self-esteem so that they could do better later on.

"Later on" rarely comes. I have seen students at the university level who couldn't understand a failing grade. "I came to class most of the time didn't I?" they pleaded. As if attendance—not mastering the material—were enough. But we all know that neither politics nor social promotion can substitute for competence. Neither will give you the skills to become a brain surgeon, a rocket scientist, an airplane pilot, or head of a company.

During World War II, the U.S. Army conducted the largest leadership study ever attempted. It was designed, implemented, and analyzed by our best and brightest professors from great universities around the country. It boiled down to a single question: "What do you really want to see in your leaders?" The answer: that the leader know his stuff.

Office politics may have gotten you promoted, but those who report to you, those who work with you, and your bosses don't care two straws about that. What they want to know is what you know and what you can do. Do you know your stuff?

Someone said you can become an expert in just about anything in about five years, if you are willing to put the time in and make the commitment. But this you must do. It is not automatic.

If you want to excel in the long run, the wisdom of the generals regarding competence is this:

* Put the time in to master your job and become expert at it.

* Your workers expect you to know your stuff, and at first line supervision, be able to teach them their jobs, if necessary.

* If you want to be an able field marshal (or general manager or CEO) then first become competent as a middle manager.

* As a competent leader, you can do good things with less-than-average employees, but if you, yourself, are incompetent, you will screw up the best of organizations.

COMMUNICATION

Battles are won through the ability of men to express concrete ideas in clear and unmistakable language.

BRIGADIER GENERAL S.L.A. MARSHALL, U.S. Army

Issuing orders is worth about 10 percent. The remaining 90 percent consists of assuring proper and vigorous execution of the order.

GENERAL GEORGE S. PATTON, JR., U.S. Army

Don't go and tell men something that you don't believe yourself, because they'll spot it and if they don't spot it at the time, they'll find out. Then you're finished.

FIELD MARSHAL SIR WILLIAM SLIM, British Army

If intercommunication between events in front and ideas behind are not maintained, then two battles will be fought—a mythical headquarters battle and an actual front-line one, in which case the real enemy is to be found in your own headquarters.

MAJOR GENERAL J.F.C. FULLER, British Army

They won't believe you if you shoot bull. When you face ranks of men and try that, you can hear 'em sigh in despair when you open your mouth, if they sense you're a phoney. . . . Maybe it doesn't sound like it, but that's an important thing in a Marine's career.

LIEUTENANT GENERAL LEWIS "CHESTY" PULLER, U.S. Marine Corps

Communication is so important, that I doubt if any of us could get anything done without it, no matter our profession, or what we are trying to do. General S.L.A. Marshall's statement about battles being won simply due to the ability to communicate is no exaggeration.

When I was a young Air Force officer, we were shown the results of an accident investigation board that had examined the crash of a transport plane. The co-pilot's father had died, and he was depressed. On take-off roll, before the aircraft lifted off, the pilot had turned to the co-pilot and said "Cheer-up!" Without thinking, the co-pilot believing he had heard the command "Gear-up!," raised the landing gear before the aircraft had left the ground.

As Patton tells us, issuing orders is only ten percent of the problem. Getting them understood and implemented is the major challenge of any leader. If you get the wrong message out, you are at war with yourself. Yet getting others to hear and understand the correct message is a lot harder than you may believe.

Do you remember the children's game, 'telephone', in which everyone sits in a circle. If you are the teacher, you begin the game by whispering a short message in the ear of the child to your left or right. That child then whispers the same message into the ear of the child sitting next to him and so on until the message comes full circle and is whispered in your ear. The amusing results are that the message you sent is never the same as the one you received. But that's just a child's game. Right?

In some of my seminars and classes on leadership, I ask the class to pick five of the most articulate communicators in the class. These ace communicators are asked to leave the room. We then ask one of these communicators to return. I read him or her a short story. I then ask this individual to name one of the other articulate communicators still outside. That individual is then asked to come in. "So and so has a little story to tell you," I announce. The first individual then tells the story to the second as best as he or she can remember it as I read it to him or her. We keep repeating the process until the final communicator tells the story to the class. It is always pretty funny, because the final story is usually nothing like the one we started with. This has been true around the country from highly competent general managers, to chiefs of police, trained in observation and memory.

We are fighting human frailties in trying to communicate, and must do everything we can do to overcome them, from sending out multiple messages, using different media, repeating the message, soliciting feedback, and spot checks as to reception.

The other critical part of our communication to subordinates is what in different ways British Field Marshal Slim and Marine General "Chesty" Puller both tell us: don't try to deceive the troops. If we do, they'll know or will find out soon enough. When that happens, they are unlikely to fully believe anything we tell them again, no matter what it is.

About communication, the wisdom of the generals says:

* To win battles, succeed in fund-raising, build a business, or succeed at anything else, you must communicate.

* Issuing orders is the easy part—the hard part is to make certain they are implemented as you want.

* If your orders are not understood and are therefore performed with errors, you are like the cartoon character Pogo, who said, "We have met the enemy and they are us."

* Don't try to fool those who would follow you by telling them something which is untrue—they'll know, or find out.

COMPETITION

A general in all of his projects should not think so much about what he wishes to do as what his enemy will do; he should never underestimate this enemy, but he should put himself in his place to appreciate difficulties and hindrances the enemy could interpose; his plans will be deranged at the slightest event if he has not foreseen everything and if he has not devised means with which to surmount the obstacles.

FREDERICK THE GREAT, German Emperor

Experienced military men are familiar with the tendency that always has to be watched in staff work, to see all our own difficulties but to credit the enemy with the ability to do things we should not dream of attempting.

MARSHAL OF THE ROYAL AIR FORCE SIR JOHN SLESSOR, Royal Air Force

In war, one sees his own troubles and not those of the enemy.

NAPOLEON BONAPARTE, French Emperor

Know the enemy and know yourself; in a hundred battles you will never be in peril. When you are ignorant of the enemy but know yourself, your chances of winning or losing are equal. If ignorant both of your enemy and of yourself, you are certain in every battle to be in peril.

SUN TZU, Ancient Chinese General

Never despise your enemy, whoever he is. Try to find out about his weapons and means, how he uses them and fights. Research into his strengths and weaknesses.

FIELD MARSHAL PRINCE ALEKSANDR V. SUVOROV, Russian Army

In any situation there are environmental variables that must be seriously considered when we plan our strategy and our actions. These variables may include the state of business and the economy, technology, available resources and know-how, governmental actions and many others including the competition. Of these, the competition is always the most serious because unlike the others it is an intelligent entity which, by definition, works contrary to our interests.

For these reasons Sun Tzu, Frederick the Great, and Prince Suvorov all agree. They tell us that it is essential to know and understand our competition, what resources are available to him and how he uses them, what his goals and objectives are, and the strategies he employs to reach them, and how he is likely to react to our planned actions. According to Sun Tzu, if we know our competitors and ourselves, we can "fight a hundred battles and never be in peril." But the reverse is also true. If we fail in understanding either our competition or ourselves, our operations will always be in peril.

The other part of the equation noted by Napoleon and by Marshal of the Royal Air Force Slessor is the tendency to assume our competition is ten feet tall, with unlimited resources, and no problems, while we are tiny, insignificant, with limited resources, but lots of problems.

Major General George B. McClellan, a Union general, was a great organizer during the Civil War. He, more than anyone else, created the Army of the Potomac and trained it from raw recruits into an efficient fighting force. But his tendency to overestimate by several magnitudes the forces under General Robert E. Lee opposing him, led him to avoid fighting and make blunder after blunder, even though his army greatly outnumbered Lee's. As a result, President Lincoln twice removed him from command, the second time permanently. McClellan simply saw his own troubles in too great of a light, and assumed his "competition" had none.

Dr. Chester Karrass, began to teach negotiation in his seminars only after studying thousands of negotiations intensely. He discovered that poor negotiators made the same mistake. They overestimated their problems which they knew, and underestimated those with whom they negotiated and did not know.

About competition, the wisdom of the generals tells us:

* ☆ In a situation in which we have one or more competitors, the competition's plans are as important as our own.
* ☆ To study our competition thoroughly in order to learn everything we can about him and how he is likely to react to our moves.
* ☆ To be aware of the tendency to overestimate our problems, while underestimating those of our competition.

COURAGE

Bravery is the capacity to perform properly even when scared half to death.

GENERAL OF THE ARMY OMAR BRADLEY, U.S. Army

The most essential qualities of a general will always be: first, a high moral courage, capable of great resolution; second a physical courage which takes no account of danger. His scientific or military acquirements are secondary to these.

GENERAL HENRI DE JOMINI, French Army, Russian Army

It doesn't do any good to fake a thing, to fake an ill or a benefit. We have to face the facts the way they are, not the way we wish they were. If we start with a false situation, then we're getting off on the wrong foot to begin with. A clear concise awareness of the exact condition, the exact problem which faces an individual, is his best weapon for coping with it.

GENERAL CURTIS E. LEMAY, U.S. Air Force

Moral courage simply means that you do what you think is right without bothering too much about the effect on yourself.

FIELD MARSHAL SIR WILLIAM SLIM, British Army

One man with courage makes a majority.

MAJOR GENERAL ANDREW JACKSON, U.S. Army

Courage does not mean that you are never afraid. Very few individuals fit this category. Sooner or later all of us are going to face a situation which downright frightens us. It need not be in battle, it could be fear of losing our job, or even fear of a new job or a new challenge.

Courage simply means that we will do what we must despite the fear. As General Bradley puts it: "perform properly even when scared half to death."

In combat, I once flew as co-pilot/navigator with a man who was known as the most courageous pilot in the squadron. He had won numerous medals for his bravery under fire. In this instance we were attacking a convoy of trucks which were defended by numerous anti-aircraft guns. He flew the aircraft and fired the weapons while I managed the fuel, made the radio calls, talked to the Forward Air Controller, and controlled the armament panel.

We rolled into the target and dived to drop our first bomb. Both of us knew that we were clearly visible to our enemies on the ground. Every gun was right on us. The sky was filled with tracers which were so close that I felt I could reach out and touch them. A single hit from 37mm cannon fire could strike a vital part of the aircraft and down us. But none hit us. As we came off target, I could see my commander was as scared as I was. He was shaking so badly, that the stick with which he controlled the aircraft was shaking too, causing the whole aircraft to shake and fly somewhat erratically. "Boy, that was awful," he said. "How many guns were there?" "I counted eight 37mm and seven ZPU," I replied. "Awful," he repeated as the aircraft shook. I thought he was going to call it a day and pull off the target. Instead, he said only, "Give me another nape (napalm)," and we rolled in again.

We kept making passes until all of the trucks were destroyed. Each time, the guns were right on us, and I could see he was at least as scared as I was, but he kept flying and fighting despite his fear.

It is rare that this kind of courage is needed in the everyday affairs of our lives. Still, it is important to have the courage that allows us to perform even though we are half scared to death. As Air Force General Curtis LeMay tells us, it does no good to ignore the problem. We have to face it with our fears and press on, no matter how difficult the situation.

The other aspect of courage I find very positive is as General "Stonewall" Jackson tells us, it only requires one individual with courage to make a majority. Recently I've been watching the TV show *West Wing* about the daily actions of the American political process, and those of the President in running the country. The show accurately depicts numerous instances where there is a serious moral dilemma, with right on one side, but some degree of right and some heavy-duty political consequences on the other. Everyone is in a twitter until one person, usually the President, but sometimes someone else, shows courage and makes the decision to do the right thing. Then, everyone else immediately falls into line, and they all seem to understand that of course that it is the right decision, and there never should have been any doubt.

Many times, this mimics real life. It only takes one person with moral courage and everyone and everything falls into line. How many other times have we seen situations where this "majority of one" was absent, and groups made grossly poor decisions, from lynchings, to the Navy's "tail-hook" scandal to the Exxon Valdez oil spill? Such incidents when the person with the moral courage was absent caused major problems, loss of respect and credibility, and even death.

Here then is the wisdom of the generals regarding courage:

* Courage doesn't mean an absence of fear—it just means performing as you should despite your fear.

* Don't wish things were different—look the issue squarely in the eye and do the hard thing anyway.

* It only takes one person with courage to make a majority.

DECEPTION

All warfare is based on deception. Hence, when able to attack, we must seem unable; when using our forces, we must seem inactive; whenever we are near, we must make the enemy believe we are far away; when far away, we must make him believe we are near. Hold out baits to entice the enemy. Feign disorder and crush him. If he is secure in all points, be prepared for him. If he is superior in strength, evade him.

SUN TZU, Ancient Chinese General

Always mystify, mislead, and surprise the enemy if possible.

LIEUTENANT GENERAL THOMAS "STONEWALL" JACKSON, Confederate States Army

Everything which the enemy least expects will succeed the best.

FREDERICK THE GREAT, German Emperor

To achieve victory we must as far as possible make the enemy blind and deaf by sealing his eyes and ears, and drive his commanders to distraction by creating confusion in their minds.

MAO TSE-TUNG, Revolutionary Head of Chinese Army

The object of the deception plan was twofold: (a) To conceal from the enemy as long as possible our intention to take the offensive (b) When this could no longer be concealed, to mislead him about both the date and the sector in which our main thrust was to be made. This was done by concealment of real intentions and real moves in the north, and by advertising false signs of activity in the south.

FIELD MARSHAL BERNARD L. MONTGOMERY, British Army

When the generals recommend deception, they do not mean deception in our dealings with customers, vendors, colleagues, friends, or family. They are talking about our competitive strategy and how it is applied. As we saw earlier, the competition is the most dangerous of all of the environmental variables because not only is it intelligent but, by definition, it competes against us and therefore works against our interests.

What the generals are saying is that all competitive strategy is based on deception; in misleading our competition as to what we are going to do until it is too late. In our eagerness to become successful, we can easily overlook the importance of deception in our strategy.

When I was boxing as a cadet, we were taught how to mislead our opponents through feints and to be careful about "telegraphing" our punches so our opponents would not know the type of punch we intended to throw and could block it or duck. There was more to boxing, we learned, than simply standing toe to toe and punching each other out.

In direct marketing, the standard test for a new product is to go slow and advertise in a limited number of media. Then, once the concept is proven profitable, to rollout with widespread advertising everywhere. Large companies are able to quickly react once they have a proven winner and may have few problems with this issue. But small entrepreneurs need to be much more creative in the use of deception in their testing. More than once, repeated advertising slowly growing over a period of months is spotted by a competitor with a larger bankroll. Not only can this competitor beat the originator to most markets with more advertising, but in some cases he can locate the source of the product, and, buying in large quantity, can sell the product at a significantly lower price.

Even large companies need to be wary in their testing in other industries, lest a competitor note their plans, and take immediate steps that will significantly impact on the potential success of these plans.

No matter what your situation, if you have competitors, take note. The wisdom of the generals on deception is:

⋆ All competitive strategy is based on deception—you must mislead the competition as to your real intentions.

⋆ Frequently, what your competition least expects will succeed best.

⋆ The key is to conceal your intentions for as long as you can—but even when your competition learns your intentions, you can mislead in other ways: timing, magnitude, duration, etc.

DECISION MAKING

In 40 hours I shall be in battle, with little information, and on the spur of the moment will have to make momentous decisions. But I believe that one's spirit enlarges with responsibility and that with God's help, I shall make them right.
GENERAL GEORGE S. PATTON, JR., U.S. Army

True decision making, by its nature, in combat and elsewhere consists in determining a line of action when choices are equally difficult.
BRIGADIER GENERAL S.L.A. MARSHALL, U.S. Army

Indecision and hesitation are fatal in any officer; in a C-in-C they are criminal.
FIELD MARSHAL BERNARD L. MONTGOMERY, British Army

Nothing is more difficult, and therefore more precious, than to be able to decide.
NAPOLEON BONAPARTE, French Emperor

Bold decisions give the best promise of success.
FIELD MARSHAL ERWIN ROMMEL, German Army

One of the most difficult things that we must learn to do in life is to make decisions. Decision-making is rarely easy, because there are usually trade-offs, advantages and disadvantages for any alternative we choose. "You've got to choose a line of action when the choices are equally difficult," says General S.L.A. Marshall. When the decision really counts, it makes it all the more difficult. This is why the Emperor Napoleon tells us quite clearly that nothing is more difficult, and therefore more valuable than to be able to decide.

Moreover, there may be danger in delay, because the world does not stop for us while we make our decisions. New factors come to bear on the situation. Customers, wives, children, competitors, may take new actions. If we wait too long, we may lose an opportunity that may never come again. "Indecision," says Field Marshal Montgomery "may be fatal."

One of my early teachers taught me that the way to train yourself to make big decisions of some importance with minimum hesitation is to train yourself by making little decisions of small importance. "Don't agonize over whether to go to the movies or study, or which movie to go to," he advised. "Consider the alternatives quickly and make your decision and move on."

Patton tells us to accept the fact that as we get more responsibility, we will have to make more important decisions. He counsels us that our ability to do this will increase with increased responsibility, and other than that, simply to trust in God. Rommel advises the decision-maker to be bold, that bold decisions succeed best.

In summary, the wisdom of the generals on decision making is:

★ Accept the fact that important decision-making is not going to be easy.

★ Recognize that once we consider the alternatives, we should not waste time, but should make the decision.

★ Bold decisions succeed better.

★ Once you have decided, don't worry as to whether you have made the right decision—trust in yourself and in God and press on!

DEFENSE

The best protection against the enemy's fire is a well-directed fire from our own guns.

ADMIRAL DAVID G. FARRAGUT, U.S. Navy

In war, the defensive exists mainly that the offensive may act more freely.

REAR ADMIRAL ALFRED MAHAN, United States Navy

There is no better way of defending a long line than by moving into the enemy's territory.

GENERAL ROBERT E. LEE, Confederate States Army

Retreat, hell! We are just attacking in another direction!

GENERAL OLIVER SMITH, U.S. Marine Corps

Little minds try to defend everything at once, but sensible people look at the main point only; they parry the worst blows and stand a little hurt if thereby they avoid a greater one. If you try and hold everything, you hold nothing.

FREDERICK THE GREAT, German Emperor

The generals know that no one can win by defense; that ultimately you must go over to the attack or perish. So, we can see by their advice that there is a predisposition against the idea of defending beginning with Admiral Farragut's assertion that the best protection against the enemy's fire is accurate fire from our own guns. And General Lee carries through with the same idea, which is an idea you may have heard before: that the best defense is a good offensive. While it would be wrong to assume you must always attack, maintaining the initiative over your competitor is a concept always worth keeping in mind.

Admiral Mahan explains that defense exists mainly so that your offense can be more effective elsewhere. This bears some thought. No one can be strong everywhere. No company, no organization, no individual, and no country. There just are never sufficient resources. That's why despite the fact that the U.S. may be the wealthiest country in the world, there are constant fights as to where to put the emphasis: defense? social welfare? law enforcement? education? All are worthy causes, but there just isn't enough money to go around. If we try to divide our resources equally among our needs, we will be weak, and probably unsuccessful everywhere. So, the idea is to put the money where it's most critical in order to accomplish our objectives, and to go "on the defensive" elsewhere. You must do the same in business. You do not have the resources to attack on all fronts, to introduce products in all markets, or to advertise in all media. So, you must pick and choose.

Frederick the Great is saying something very similar when he says that small minds try to defend everywhere. It just can't be done. So the good military, business, or life strategist will pick those areas that are most critical. We can call them "decisive points." Resources will be concentrated at these "decisive points" for either defense or offense.

Marine General Smith's comment tells us that a strategic retreat or withdrawal, which may be equated with a defensive strategy, may be accompanied by a tactical attack. For example, the decision to withdraw a product from your line (defense) may be accompanied by an intense advertising campaign (attack) to sell all of this product that you can at full price.

Here is the wisdom of the generals regarding defense:

* ★ It is possible that the best defense you can devise is to go on the offensive—always consider this option.
* ★ Defense can and should be used in conjunction with offensive operations.
* ★ Don't try to defend everywhere—you can't do it—put your resources on the critical points to accomplish your objectives.
* ★ A strategic defense may require a tactical offense.

DELEGATION

Be content to do what you can for the well-being of what properly belongs to you; commit the rest to those who are responsible.

GENERAL ROBERT E. LEE, Confederate States Army

The man who cannot bring himself to trust the judgment and good faith of other men cannot command very long. He will soon break under the unnecessary strain he puts on himself.

BRIGADIER GENERAL S.L.A. MARSHALL, U.S. Army

I never knew what to do with a paper except to put it in a side pocket or pass it to a clerk who understood it better than I did.

GENERAL ULYSSES S. GRANT, U.S. Army

I was present at the attack near the monastery of Svyanty Kryzh, but held my tongue, not wishing in the least to detract from the praise-worthy, skillful and brave commands of my subordinates.

FIELD MARSHAL PRINCE ALEKSANDR V. SUVOROV, Russian Army

They also knew that I trusted them to carry out their missions with an absolute minimum of interference. The field assignments were theirs, and my philosophy (as each commander understood) was that they would handle them best.

MAJOR GENERAL ARIEL SHARON, Army of Israel

If you are to manage operations requiring the efforts of more than a single individual, you will soon discover that you cannot do everything yourself. You must delegate your authority and rely on others. Note that I said delegate your authority, for there is no way you can delegate responsibility. It will always be yours.

Many managers find that this is not always so easy to do. You advance because you were good at what you were doing. If you are a new manager, you have probably gained quite a proficiency at doing things . . . all things . . . by yourself. Even if you are an experienced manager and supervisor, there are some things that you can probably do better than anyone else. Because of this, if one of your followers has difficulty with some task, it is very tempting to simply take over and do what needs to be done. The generals tell us that we should resist this temptation. If you do not, the one who should be doing this job will never learn to do it properly. He or she will never improve and will always rely on you. Moreover, as General Marshall says, you will eventually break under the strain.

Some managers are afraid to trust their people. But you must. Take General Lee's advice, and you do your job of managing. Let others, experts in their field or those with other responsibilities under you, do theirs. Israeli General Sharon was frequently right up front with his men. He successfully led major forces against the Egyptians in both the Six Day War of 1967 and the Yom Kippur War of 1973. Yet, he trusted his subordinate commanders to accomplish the tasks he set for them with minimum interference. To do otherwise is known as "micro-management," perhaps the greatest enemy of effective, creative management. If you properly train those who report to you so that you can delegate to them freely, you can be like General Grant, and leave the details to the experts with complete trust, so that you can proceed to win the war.

One final point. As noted earlier, you delegate authority but retain responsibility. What this means is this. If things go right you give full credit to those under you who did the job. Should things go wrong, you may not say, "Oh it was so and so's fault. I gave him the job." You delegated authority, not responsibility. So when things go wrong, the responsibility is still yours, and you must accept it and never blame others.

About delegation, the wisdom of the generals is:

* Learn to delegate to others—otherwise you'll eventually crack.

* Do your job and let those who report to you do their jobs with minimum interference.

★ Train your followers so that you can trust them to do any job you delegate to them.

★ You delegate authority, not responsibility.

★ If things go right, others should get the credit—if they go wrong, the responsibility is yours, you must accept the blame.

DEPRESSION

It ain't as bad as you think. It will look better in the morning.

GENERAL COLIN POWELL, U.S. Army

I have always believed that a motto for generals must be "no regrets," "no crying over spilt milk."

FIELD MARSHAL SIR WILLIAM SLIM, British Army

A battle is lost less through the loss of men than by discouragement.

FREDERICK THE GREAT, German Emperor

Even the final decision of a war is not to be regarded as absolute. The conquered nation often sees it only as a passing evil, to be repaired in after times by political combinations.

MAJOR GENERAL KARL VON CLAUSEWITZ, Prussian Army

Never take counsel of your fears.

LIEUTENANT GENERAL THOMAS JACKSON, Confederate States Army

We all face depression at one time or another. The generals tell us that for the sake of performance, we must overcome this depression. As Frederick the Great notes, a battle is lost less through the loss of men than by discouragement. This is echoed by "Stonewall" Jackson who advises us never to take counsel of our fears. This is not so easy to do because, "fatigue makes cowards of us all."

How can we overcome discouragement and depression, especially when we are tired and under a great deal of stress? One way is simply to recognize that things will get better. In fact, as General Colin Powell points out, sometimes things aren't as bad as we think at all, its only our way of looking at it.

Once I gave an all-day seminar and collected evaluations of my performance afterward. Though extremely tired and fatigued, I looked at these evaluations just before going to sleep and was horrified. It seemed to be that the comments were very negative. I went to sleep depressed and feeling I had let my client down and not done the job for which I was paid.

The next morning after breakfast, in following Clausewitz's advice about even the final decision of war as being absolute, and Slim's statement about not crying over spilt milk, I picked up the evaluations again. I thought I would make notes to see what I should change and how I could improve. I was amazed to see that 99% of the evaluations were very positive and complimentary. Only one individual was critical. There was nothing for me to change! Later in the day, I received a call from my client congratulating me on "the best seminar" his company had ever received. It is strange the tricks your mind can play on you when you are tired. Yes, the situation frequently looks a lot better in the morning.

So here's what the wisdom of the generals says about depression:

* Depression is serious stuff and can cause you to lose your battle.
* Don't make important decisions while in a depressed or discouraged state.
* Don't cry over spilt milk.
* No matter what has happened, the situation isn't final.
* Tomorrow, things are going to look better.

DOUBT

Of the many harms that can beset an army, vacillation is the greatest. Of the disasters that can befall an army, none surpasses doubt.

GENERAL (TAI KUNG) CHIANG SHANG, Ancient Chinese General

An irresolute general . . . although at the head of an army superior in number to that of the enemy, finds himself always inferior on the field of battle.

NAPOLEON BONAPARTE, French Emperor

The fellow who "doesn't know" has caused a great deal of harm. Arrest for the officer who "doesn't know" and house arrest for the field or general officer.

FIELD MARSHAL ALEKSANDR V. SUVOROV, Russian Army

You must not retain for one instant any man in a responsible position when you have become doubtful of his ability to do the job.

GENERAL OF THE ARMY DWIGHT D. EISENHOWER, U.S. Army

I thought momentarily of these three submarines, traversing another 3000 miles of hostile seas before sneaking along the Empire to its very back door. Then I checked myself; such thoughts were timid. Here I had command of the best fighting ship ever built, capable of going anywhere and sinking any enemy ship. With complete confidence, I reached for the Night Order Book.

REAR ADMIRAL RICHARD H. O'KANE, U.S. Navy

The great enemy in our goal of accomplishing any task or worthwhile project is doubt. How many times have we imagined great projects and achievements only to discard them as the "reality" of doubt set in and we dwelt on all the reasons why we could not succeed? Tai Kung Chiang Shang's words ring as true today as they did thousands of years ago: "Of the disasters that can befall an army, none surpasses doubt."

Doubt destroys our resolution to such an extent, that Napoleon tells us that even though we may have superior resources to that of a competitor, doubt will still make us inferior in the competition that takes place in the marketplace. And Field Marshal Suvorov says that doubt expressed by an officer is so serious that even if a general or field marshal, he should be arrested.

But what if we have real doubts? How should we proceed? General Eisenhower makes it clear when he recommends getting rid of a subordinate in a responsible position about whom we have doubts. We should not allow the doubts to overwhelm us so that we tell ourselves that our goal or object is impossible. Nor should we execute a plan while still filled with doubt that we can succeed. The real lesson from Eisenhower's recommendation is that we must resolve these doubts before proceeding. If we doubt an individual's ability to get the job done, we can and must remove that individual from the responsible position that he or she holds. Eisenhower felt so strongly about this that he felt that Robert E. Lee's greatest error at Gettysburg was failing to relieve his otherwise highly effective deputy, James Longstreet, when Longstreet expressed doubt that Picket's Charge could succeed.

Admiral O'Kane gives us another way of resolving our doubts before action. O'Kane was executive officer of one of the most celebrated submarines of World War II, the U.S.S. Wahoo. Later, he became captain of another highly successful sub, the U.S.S. Tang. For his World War II exploits on these two submarines, O'Kane earned the Congressional Medal of Honor, three Navy Crosses and numerous other decorations. Yet, even this heroic boat captain had doubts. What did he do? I checked myself, he says. "Such thoughts were timid. Here I had command of the best fighting ship ever built, capable of going anywhere and sinking any enemy ship. With complete confidence, I reached for the Night Order Book." In other words, we can also remove doubt by reviewing and dwelling on all the reasons we will succeed, rather than the obstacles to our success.

About doubt, the wisdom of the generals tells us:

* ✭ It is one of the greatest harms that can get in the way of our success.

* ✭ We must not permit it to exist in ourselves or in those that work for us.

* ✭ If necessary, be prepared to get rid of doubters in responsible positions.

* ✭ Dwell on the reasons why you will succeed rather than the obstacles to your success.

DUTY

All men are afraid in battle. The coward is the one who lets his fear overcome his sense of duty.
GENERAL GEORGE S. PATTON, JR., U.S. Army

The brave man inattentive to his duty is worth little more to his country than the coward who deserts in the hour of danger.
MAJOR GENERAL ANDREW JACKSON, U.S. Army

Do your duty in all things . . . You cannot do more, you should never wish to do less.
GENERAL ROBERT E. LEE, Confederate States Army

England expects every man to do his duty.
ADMIRAL LORD HORATIO NELSON, Royal Navy

The only policy in high positions is an intense devotion to duty and the unswerving pursuit of the target, in spite of criticism—whispered or in the open.
FIELD MARSHAL BERNARD MONTGOMERY, British Army

Duty is the action required by one's position, profession, or task. The generals impart to it an almost mystical quality of very high importance. Perhaps this is because the tasks we require of our soldiers, sailors, airmen, and marines are of such magnitude and at such risk that it makes duty all the more difficult to fulfill and the consequences of not fulfilling it all the more devastating. But the importance of the concept is easily broadened to all professions from law and medicine to business and sports.

I recall when doing extensive modernizing of our home several years ago, how much in legal fees, time and money wasted, not to mention ill-will would never have happened had a sub-contractor simply done his duty. But as Patton says, some let their fear of loss, whether life or money, or ridicule, overcome their sense of duty. And, so, they fail.

Field Marshal Montgomery says we must do our duty irrespective of fear, and criticism whether spoken or whispered. So, perhaps duty should have a mystical quality of great importance for all of us, no matter our occupation or our objectives.

It doesn't matter how brilliant or capable an individual is if he or she fails to do what is required. They might just as well be stupid and incapable. The results are the same. "England expects every man to do his duty," signaled Admiral Nelson to his fleet before the Battle of Trafalgar. If we are to be successful, life expects the same from all of us, man or woman regardless of our pursuits.

The wisdom of the generals regarding duty is:

★ Sense of duty can overcome fear.

★ A brilliant, capable individual who fails to do his duty is no better than one who is stupid and incapable.

★ If you want to succeed, always do the duty which your position, profession, or task requires.

ENDURANCE

The first virtue in a soldier is endurance of fatigue; courage is only the second virtue.

NAPOLEON BONAPARTE, French Emperor

There is no quicker way to lose a battle than to lose it on the road for lack of adequate hardening of the troops.

BRIGADIER GENERAL S.L.A. MARSHALL, U.S. Army

You have to lead men in war by requiring more from the individual than he thinks he can do.

GENERAL OF THE ARMY GEORGE C. MARSHALL, U.S. Army

Work hard to keep fit. That little extra stamina may some day pull you out of some deep holes.

GENERAL MATTHEW B. RIDGWAY, U.S. Army

A pint of sweat will save a gallon of blood.

GENERAL GEORGE S. PATTON, JR., U.S. Army

I once read about a famous business executive who was asked the secret of his incredible success. "Simple," he said. "I work several hours longer than any of my competitors each day. In a year's time, I have put in a couple of months of additional work."

To put in that kind of a workday may not be your cup of tea. But I have never known anyone successful who did not occasionally have to put in much longer and harder hours than a "standard" forty hour work week or eight hour work day. You can't do this, even on an irregular basis, unless you have developed the endurance. Not only will you not be able to think clearly, and likely make poor decisions and do less than your normal standard of work, you also risk a heart attack and a whole pack of other ailments. And that's no exaggeration.

About twenty years ago, the Air Force decided to change its way of physical testing. Since airmen have such varying schedules, they usually can't exercise together as do the members of the other services. So it was decided to adopt something called the 5BX, or five basic exercises which originated with the Royal Canadian Air Force. This system allowed each person to work at his or her own pace to reach a certain level. The assumption was that people would work out on their own and would eventually reach the level of physical fitness desired. The Air Force decided to give everyone a year to reach that level, and then would spot check during unscheduled organizational readiness inspections.

While everyone started with a great deal of enthusiasm, many "fell off the wagon" and quit working out. Came the unscheduled, unannounced readiness inspections and spot checks, not only did many individuals fail, but some actually had heart attacks while trying to demonstrate levels of fitness for which they were not prepared. That program was dropped and a different program of planned testing re-initiated.

So how can you prepare yourself to outwork the competition on either a regular or "as needed" basis? As Patton says, "A pint of sweat will save a gallon of blood." To do this you must in turn follow General Ridgway's advice: "Work hard to keep fit. That little extra stamina may some day pull you out of some deep holes."

About endurance and fitness, the wisdom of the generals is:

★ You must work on a regular basis to become and maintain fitness and have the endurance you need for success

★ Have the endurance, and you can easily outwork the competition and when necessary pull yourself out of some deep holes.

ENTHUSIASM

In all men there is an innate excitability and drive which is kindled by the heat of the fight, and it is the function of the general not to quench but to heighten the excitement.

JULIUS CAESAR, Ancient Roman General and Emperor

I already knew that even in the ordinary condition of the mind enthusiasm is a potent element with soldiers, but what I saw that day convinced me that if it can be excited from a state of despondency its power is almost irresistible.

GENERAL PHILIP H. SHERIDAN, U.S. Army

Shrewd critics have assigned military success to all manner of things—tactics, shape of frontiers, speed, happily placed rivers, mountains or woods, intellectual ability, or the use of artillery. All in a measure true, but none vital. The secret lies in the inspiring spirit which lifted weary, footsore men out of themselves and made them march forgetful of agony.

GENERAL GEORGE S. PATTON, JR., U.S. Army

In a word, by exciting their enthusiasm by every means in harmony with their tone of mind . . . we may maintain a high military spirit.

GENERAL HENRI DE JOMINI, French Army, Russian Army

I wanted to imbue my crews with enthusiasm and a complete faith in their army and to instill in them a spirit of selfless readiness to serve in it. Only those possessed of such a spirit could hope to succeed in the grim realities of submarine warfare. Professional skill alone would not survive.

GRAND ADMIRAL KARL DONITZ, German Navy

There is no question that enthusiasm is a powerful force which is capable of greatly increasing the desire to attain any goal or objective. General Sheridan knew what he was talking about. On one occasion, his mere presence on the battlefield turned everything around. Sheridan found he could turn despondency into victory through enthusiasm for the job. Yet, there are leaders, in and out of the military, whose idea of leadership is staying cool and aloof. This surprises me. Sure you need to be cool inside to make the right decisions under stress. And when everything is falling to pieces, staying cool "under fire" can be inspirational. But analytical decisions made in a quiet, paneled, air conditioned room (or underground bunker) and passed on to others to carry them out will hardly elicit excitement or enthusiasm.

Forgetting the problems associated in communicating with others through several channels which we discussed earlier, do these leaders really believe that anyone is interested in following their decisions simply because they make them? Are their egos so inflated, or the belief in the power of their offices and positions so great that they think this fact will substitute for enthusiasm or create it? There is no way for this to happen.

How can we create enthusiasm? My friend, multimillionaire Joe Cossman said that when he was a door-to-door vacuum salesman prior to World War II, they would begin each day with a half-hour of singing before making sales calls. Billionaire W. Clement Stone says make three statements out loud and with enthusiasm: "I feel happy! I feel healthy! I feel terrific!" Keep repeating these words until you believe it. I've found that explaining the situation, what you're trying to do, why you are doing it, how you are going to do it, and the benefits that will accrue after it is done helps get people worked up. And make no mistake, if you aren't enthusiastic, no one else will be either.

The wisdom of the generals about enthusiasm is this:

* Enthusiasm is a powerful force that can cause an unconquerable spirit to help you accomplish any task or reach any goal.

* It is one of your functions to create this force, either in yourself alone, or in others.

EXAMPLE

Officers of the Israeli army do not send their men into battle. They lead them into battle.

LIEUTENANT GENERAL MOSHE DAYAN, ARMY OF ISRAEL

The power of example is very important to people under stress.

GENERAL SIR JOHN HACKETT, British Army

I kept thinking of the time when I'd ordered a change in tactics when we were going to hit St. Nazaire, late in 1942. It was the first time in the Army Air Force's European Theater experience that a large formation of heavy bombers had ever approached a target without using evasive action in an attempt to avoid the enemy's ground-to-air shellfire. I led that one, so I didn't have to suffer and wonder, off somewhere in the distance. I suffered and wondered right there, twenty-two thousand feet above St. Nazaire.

GENERAL CURTIS E. LeMAY, U.S. Air Force

Clearchos . . . marched with the army in battle order, himself commanding the rearguard. They came on ditches and canals full of water, which they could not cross without bridges; but they managed by making bridges of fallen date-palms or others which they cut down. Then one could learn what a commander Clearchos was. In his left hand he held the spear, a stick in his right; and if he thought there was any shirking, he picked out the right man and gave him one, and also he lent a hand himself, jumping into the mud, so that all were ashamed not to work as hard as he did. Those of thirty years and under were tolled off for the job; but when they saw how keen Clearchos was, the older men helped.

XENOPHON, Ancient Greek General

I used to say to them, "go boldly in among the English," and then I used to go boldly in myself.

JOAN OF ARC, French Army

There was once a game we played as children. You may remember it. It was called follow the leader. Those that followed had to do whatever the leader did, no matter how daring or dangerous. How many followed simply because they were ashamed not to? That is the power of example.

Lieutenant General Jay Kelley, then commander of Air University said, "We can tell our young officers what to do and they may or may not do it. But it's just like raising kids. They watch what we do. They may or may not do what we say, but they will always do what we do." This means that we must not only set the example in what we want others who follow us to do, but we must avoid doing what we don't want them to do.

Israeli Army leaders say that setting the example is one of their secrets of success. In other armies, officers are taught not to lead from the absolute front. That is because you can control the situation better by advancing one echelon back from the front, and also if your officers are always in the front of a unit, the casualty rate among the leaders is enormous. The Israeli Army understands this, but they tell their officers to lead from the front anyway. They feel that the importance of the example is the overriding issue.

I often wondered about Joan of Arc. How did this young girl achieve such amazing success? When she took over the French Army, it had tried to raise the siege of Orleans for eight months unsuccessfully. Joan took command and raised the siege in eight days. Her secret was using the example. She had a banner made which clearly identified her. She told her soldiers that the way to win was to go where the action was. Then she led by going where the action was herself.

General LeMay was a colonel when he took it upon himself to overrule experts who had already flown combat in Europe. They told him that if his bombers flew straight and level for more than a few minutes, they would get shot out of the sky. The problem was, by not flying straight and level, they rarely hit their targets. He calculated that overall they would lose more aircraft because they would have to keep returning to targets which were not destroyed than if they took their lumps and got it right the first time. But he knew he was asking his airmen to do something they had been told was suicide. So, he flew the first "straight and level" mission himself. It wasn't suicide, and the U.S. Army Air Force adopted LeMay's tactics thereafter.

About the example the wisdom of the generals is:

* ★ Don't tell people to do difficult things—set the example and do it yourself.

* ★ Others don't follow what you say so much as what they watch you do.

* ★ Don't do what you want others not to do and do what you want them to do.

EXPLOITATION OF SUCCESS

Next to victory, the act of pursuit is the most important in war.

MAJOR GENERAL KARL VON CLAUSEWITZ, Prussian Army

Strenuous, unrelaxing pursuit is therefore as imperative after a battle as courage during it.

REAR ADMIRAL ALFRED T. MAHAN, U.S. Navy

Once the enemy has been thoroughly beaten up, success can be exploited by attempting to overrun and destroy major parts of disorganized formations. Here again, speed is everything. The enemy must never be allowed time to reorganize.

FIELD MARSHAL ERWIN ROMMEL, German Army

When we have incurred the risk of a battle, we should know how to profit by the victory, and not merely content ourselves, according to custom, with possession of the field.

FIELD MARSHAL MAURICE COMTE DE SAXE, French Army

A pursuit gives even cowards confidence.

XENOPHON, Ancient Greek General

There is a natural, human tendency which can cheat us of our full success. This tendency occurs when we are already winning and have achieved partial success. The tendency is to let up and rest. We are tired. Everything has been going okay. Why be greedy? Why not take a break? We can get the rest of what we want tomorrow.

The wisdom of the generals tells us to resist this tendency. The problem with delay is manifold. Any situation is constantly changing. The elements that are enabling us to win today may not be present tomorrow. Delay allows our competition to regroup and have the opportunity to develop and implement a new strategy. Maybe our competitor will receive additional resources unavailable today. Other aspects of the environment could change by tomorrow. The government could pass a law limiting what we are doing. A cheaper material or process could become available making our product obsolete. Our target market may become more interested in an alternative product or service.

Moreover, there are other advantages to continuing to press our advantages. We may be very tired and would like a rest after the strenuous efforts which brought us to where we are now. However, our competition is even more tired, and being on the defensive, feels this to a much greater extent than we do. As Xenophon notes, even our "cowards" feel confident when we are on the offensive. The same may be extrapolated where we are just talking about an individual. The fear within ourselves is barely felt when we are winning and moving towards full victory in a project, task, or career. We just don't know what the situation will be in the future.

I advise job seekers who come off an outstanding interview and are certain of an offer which has not yet been made to continue to proceed as if no offer were forthcoming. Once a good friend was in this mode. He was led to believe an offer as company president would be made within two weeks time. I practically begged him to continue his campaign. I couldn't convince him. The two weeks stretched into many weeks. Still he was strung along. In the end, the presidency of this privately owned firm was given to the owner's son, and my friend had to re-open his campaign after the trail had grown cold.

For all of these reasons, many aspects of our success, which contribute to our winning today, may not be available in the future. So after all the trouble and investment we made to win, we want to exploit this to the fullest.

The wisdom of the generals pertaining to exploitation of success is:

* You never know what your situation may be in the future; the elements that caused or assisted in your success may not be present.

* When you are winning, you have the advantage; don't slack off until full victory has been attained.

FAILURE

A lost battle is a battle one thinks one has lost.

FIELD MARSHAL FERDINAND FOCH, French Army

He who in war fails to do what he undertakes, may always plead the accidents which invariably attend military affairs: but he who declares a thing to be impossible, which is subsequently accomplished, registers his own incapacity.

FIELD MARSHAL ARTHUR WELLESLEY, The Duke of Wellington, British Army

The history of failure in war can be summed up in two words: too late. Too late in comprehending the deadly purpose of a potential enemy; too late in realizing the mortal danger; too late in preparedness; too late in uniting all possible forces for resistance; too late in standing with one's friends.

GENERAL OF THE ARMY DOUGLAS MACARTHUR, U.S. Army

I claim we got a hell of a beating. We got run out of Burma and it is humiliating as hell. I think we ought to find out what caused it, and go back and retake it.

GENERAL JOSEPH STILWELL, U.S. Army

The service cannot afford to keep a man who does not succeed.

LIEUTENANT GENERAL THOMAS JACKSON, Confederate States Army

We are all going to have failures at one time or another—that's the nature of life. What we want to do is to minimize failure and maximize success. That's what this lesson from the wisdom of generals is about.

First of all, failure starts in the mind. You know as well as I do that there have been times when you have failed at something even before you have begun, or certainly before all the results are in. That's what Field Marshal Foch is talking about when he says that a lost battle is one that you think you have lost. If you think you have lost in any situation, I guarantee you that you are right.

The Duke of Wellington lays it out by saying that there will always be reasons why you may not succeed, reasons over which you have little control. However, when you start by assuming something to be impossible, there is no way you are going to be successful. Interestingly, what one person says is impossible to accomplish, another gets done. We see that all the time.

Before Roger Bannister managed to run a mile in four minutes, just about everyone said it was impossible. Doctors and physiologists "proved" that the human organism just was not constructed to move that fast. Then, Roger Bannister did it. As soon as others saw that it could be done, many followed. Today even high school athletes reach this goal, and the world's record for the mile is much faster.

This is not much different from MacArthur's comments regarding what leads to failure: too little, too late. There is a sequence of events leading to failure just as there is a sequence leading to success. It starts with the state of mind. If you haven't made up your mind that you can and will succeed, then the actions you take, your performance along the way, fall right into line and take you to failure.

But as I said earlier, we're not talking about permanent failure. Everyone has temporary failures, successful people call them setbacks. We can recognize the fact that we got clobbered. It's what we do afterwards that counts. Do we pick ourselves up and immediately get right back into action? That's what General Stilwell recommends. That's what leads to ultimate success.

Failure can be an important lesson leading to even greater success. I've heard of many highly successful people that "failed their way to success." R.H. Macy, who founded Macy's Department Store failed with four previous stores. Ultimately a store he started was wildly successful. That's true with a lot of people. But for those that give up and accept failure? As "Stonewall" Jackson notes, we can't afford generals who don't succeed, and in our lives we cannot afford and should not tolerate less than success either—we don't have to.

The wisdom of the generals regarding failure is:

* ✶ It all starts with the mind—if we think "failure" that's what we're going to achieve.
* ✶ Nothing permitted by the laws of nature is impossible.
* ✶ We must prepare for success ahead of time by the actions we take.
* ✶ Failure is temporary; it can and should be only a lesson on the way to success.

FEAR

All men are frightened. The more intelligent they are, the more they are frightened. The courageous man is the man who forces himself, in spite of his fear, to carry on.
                    GENERAL GEORGE S. PATTON, JR., U.S. Army

Fear is the beginning of wisdom.
                    GENERAL WILLIAM T. SHERMAN, U.S. Army

The man afraid wants to do nothing; indeed he does not care even to think of taking action.
                    BRIGADIER GENERAL S.L.A. MARSHALL, U.S. Army

Fear unhinges the will, and by unhinging the will it paralyzes the reason; thoughts are dispersed in all directions in place of being concentrated on one definite aim . . . Whilst moral fear is largely overcome by courage based on reason, physical fear is overcome by courage based on physical means.
                    MAJOR GENERAL J.F.C. FULLER, British Army

In time of battle, when victory hangs in the balance, it is necessary to put down any sign of weakness, indecision, lack of aggressiveness or panic, whether the man wears stars on his shoulders or chevrons on his sleeve, for one frightened soldier can infect his whole unit.

                    GENERAL MATTHEW B. RIDGWAY, U.S. Army

I don't think anyone would dare call Patton a coward. Yet, this bravest of men says quite clearly that all men are frightened at times. All men or women have fear. It's what you do with that fear that counts.

In fact, fear can even be positive. That's General Sherman's point in stating it is the beginning of wisdom. We can learn from what has caused the fear and avoid or eliminate a potentially dangerous threat. Fear may also be useful in what it causes us to do. A scene in the movie "The Great Santini" illustrates this point. The Marine Corps lieutenant colonel, played by Robert Duvall who is the protagonist says: "Yes I am afraid. That's what makes me such a great pilot."

General Marshall points out the great danger in fear. It can paralyze us and prevent us from taking essential action. General Fuller continues this theme by explaining that fear paralyzes the reason and prevents the mind from concentrating on the objective. However, Fuller also shows us how to overcome this fear: moral fear by reasoning and physical fear by taking action.

In situations of stress, you cannot permit others to outwardly demonstrate the effects of the very real fear that everyone is probably feeling, because such a demonstration creates panic and can paralyze your entire organization. That's the time when you must set the example by your own demeanor and, if necessary, speak the words, or take the actions to help this individual get control.

The wisdom of the generals about fear is:

* Everyone has fear—it is what we do with our fear that counts.

* Fear can paralyze us from taking action and prevent us from focusing on the objective—but it can also be overcome through reason and action.

* We cannot permit others to demonstrate the effects of fear during times of stress because it causes panic which can spread throughout our organization.

FLEXIBILITY

We must make allowance for delays and difficulties . . .

GENERAL ROBERT E. LEE, Confederate States Army

Learn to make dispositions in such a fashion that the fate of your army does not depend on the good or bad conduct of a single minor officer.

FREDERICK THE GREAT, German Emperor

They planned their campaigns just as you might make a splendid set of harness. It looks very well; and answers very well; until it gets broken; and then they are done for. Now I make my campaigns of ropes. If anything went wrong, I tied a knot; and went on.

FIELD MARSHAL ARTHUR WESSELEY, The Duke of Wellington, British Army

Unhappy the general who comes on the field of battle with a system.

NAPOLEON BONAPARTE, French Emperor

Every Red Army commander must firmly grasp the fact that slavery to routine and extreme enthusiasm for some specific plan or some specific method are the most dangerous thing for all of us . . . nothing can be absolute or solidly fixed; everything flows and changes, and any means, any methods might be used in a certain situation.

GENERAL MIKHAIL V. FRUNZE, Soviet Army

An old military saying says that everything that can go wrong, will go wrong. This cautions the military commander to be prepared for the worst, not to put too much reliance on any one element, and to be flexible.

Robert E. Lee tells us that we must not assume that everything will go perfectly, exactly as planned, because it will not. So if we are to be flexible, we must think ahead as to what we will do under a variety of failures and eventualities.

When I am speaking, or giving a seminar I frequently use Powerpoint™ as the planned vehicle for illustrating my presentation.

Should that fail, I have overhead backups. I also have handouts with reproductions of each overhead. And finally, I am mentally prepared that if I have nothing, I can still give my talk or presentation without any visual assistance at all. At one time or another I have had to use all of these options, and I am always ready to do so.

Frederick the Great goes one step further in warning not to rely too much on one individual for the success of your endeavor, either. Are you still ready to make a group presentation if one or more members comes late or fails to show? Are you prepared to cover for him or her? You should be.

The Duke of Wellington, Napoleon, and General Frunze are all in agreement in cautioning us about relying too much on a fixed and rigid system of operation. If we are in a competition and always do the same thing, you can bet that after several repetitions our competitor will know exactly what we are going to do and will have effective counter-moves prepared. However, even with the best prepared system, with no competition, something can easily go amiss. If our overall plan is based on everything working in a certain way from start to finish, we've got real problems.

I am a strong proponent of extensive planning for every activity, marketing, business, and projects. But one of the advantages in the preparations of these plans is the thinking that goes into them including potential threats, problems and opportunities that may occur on the way to reach our goals and what we will do about them.

The wisdom of the generals on flexibility is this:

* Everything that can go wrong will go wrong—prepare for it.

* Don't depend too much on any one individual in your plans.

* Don't implement a plan that's fixed in concrete.

* Be prepared to avoid the threats, take care of the problems and take advantage of the opportunities.

* Stay flexible!

GOALS

*P*ursue one great decisive aim with force and determination . . .

MAJOR GENERAL KARL VON CLAUSEWITZ, Prussian Army

*T*he man who tries to hang on to everything ends up by
holding nothing.

FREDERICK THE GREAT, German Emperor

*M*any good generals exist in Europe, but they see too many things
at once: I see but one thing, and that is the masses; I seek to destroy
them, sure that the minor matters will fall of themselves.

NAPOLEON BONAPARTE, French Emperor

*O*ther great difficulties, experienced by every great general, are to
measure truly the thousand and one reports that come to him in the
midst of conflict; to preserve a clear and well-defined purpose at every
instant of time, and to cause all efforts to converge on that end.

GENERAL WILLIAM T SHERMAN, U.S. Army

*I*n selecting the proper objective the air leader must consider not
alone his capacity and his own desires, but he must consider the mission
of the ground forces and the concerted effort and plan of the whole force.

GENERAL OF THE AIR FORCE HENRY H. ARNOLD, U.S. Air Force

W hy don't we reach the goals we set for ourselves? There may be
many reasons, but General Clausewitz and Emperor Frederick
point out an important one: we try to go after too many things at once,
rather than attacking these goals sequentially. General Clausewitz recommends that we pursue one decisive goal with everything we've got.
Frederick the Great's statement that if you'll try to hang onto everything, you'll probably end up with nothing is an appropriate corollary.

Dr. Charles Garfield, a psychologist who studied peak performers
and highly successful people found that one major difference between
them and others less successful was that they concentrated on one main

goal while others dissipated their efforts going after many goals at the same time. Napoleon Hill, that famed philosopher of success commissioned by steel magnate Andrew Carnegie to uncover the secrets of high success found the same. He called it deciding and acting on a definite purpose. Answering someone who proudly told Garfield how many goals he could juggle successfully at work simultaneously, Garfield responded, "Don't juggle, choose."

As the Emperor Napoleon instructs us, worry about the big things in our situation. The small things will take care of themselves. General Sherman points out that this isn't so easy to do because you will be confronted with countless distractions. However, if you are to be a "great general," then you must "preserve a clear and well-defined purpose at every instant of time, cause all efforts to converge on that end."

About goals, the wisdom we learn from the generals is:

* Focus all your efforts on your main goal.

* Don't be distracted—focus your efforts on a clear and well-defined purpose.

* Concentrate on the big things—the small things will take care of themselves.

HOPE

A leader is a dealer in hope.

NAPOLEON BONAPARTE, Emperor of France

Hope encourages men to endure and attempt everything; in depriving them of it, or in making it too distant, you deprive them of their very soul.

FIELD MARSHAL MAURICE COMTE DE SAXE, French Army

The principle task of the general is mental . . .

FREDERICK THE GREAT, German Emperor

Put your trust in God, my boys, and keep your powder dry!

OLIVER CROMWELL, English Army

It can be done.

GENERAL COLIN POWELL, U.S. Army

Hope is nothing more than desire accompanied by expectations that our desire will be fulfilled. Hope is required not only of the military leader, but for all of us. Were it not for hope, Henry Ford would have died an obscure mechanic. We would never have heard of the Wright Brothers, either. They would have continued to repair bicycles. Without hope, Bill Gates would have stayed at Harvard, graduated, and would probably be working for one of the companies in Silicon Valley, most likely not as president.

Hope encourages men to endure and attempt everything Field Marshal de Saxe assures us, and indeed, the task of the general is therefore mental advises Frederick the Great.

So never, never discourage hope in the interests of making others "face reality." That's just plain stupid. You never know what is possible. You're not God. Doctors are daily amazed by cures of incurable diseases that aren't supposed to happen. But they do happen and so frequently that they finally gave it a scientific sounding name: spontaneous remission. That just means the doctors don't know what happened.

It used to be that doctors would tell you the bad news: "Sorry, Mr. Jones or Ms. Smith you only have a 5% chance of surviving." "Gee, that's swell, doc. I have no hope. I might as well hang it up right now." Don't forget what Harrison Ford told us as Han Solo when greatly outnumbered and under fire from Empire fighters? "Never tell me the odds."

Maybe *Star Wars* is only a movie, but as I said earlier, many doctors won't tell you the facts in quite this way any more. Rather, they will emphasize that if you are in the 5% cure group, that figure is 100% as far as you are concerned. Now this does not mean if we want something to happen, we need to do nothing at all. That's the point of Oliver Cromwell's assertion. However, we are all dealers in hope, and must be if we are to be successful. Yes, General Powell, "It can be done."

* We are all dealers in hope.

* Don't destroy anyone's hope, especially not your own.

* It can be done.

HUMOR

A sense of humor is part of the art of leadership, of getting along with people, of getting things done.

GENERAL OF THE ARMY DWIGHT D. EISENHOWER, U.S. Army

To speak of the importance of a sense of humor would be futile, if it were not that what cramps so many men isn't that they are by nature humorless as they are hesitant to exercise what humor they possess.

BRIGADIER GENERAL S.L.A. MARSHALL, U.S. Army

Humor is an effective but tricky technique in command and leadership, beneficial when used wisely, but it can backfire into a dangerous booby-trap if overworked or crudely employed.

MAJOR GENERAL AUBREY NEWMAN, U.S. Army

Most of the time, leaders should laugh at themselves rather than others.

MAJOR GENERAL PERRY M. SMITH, U.S. Air Force

When things are going badly in battle the best tonic is to take one's mind off one's own troubles by considering what a rotten time one's opponent must be having.

FIELD MARSHAL ARCHIBALD WAVELL, British Army

We don't all have a sense of humor such that we can keep those that work with us in stitches. We shouldn't use this talent for this purpose even if we had it. In fact, you don't need to be a comedian to show you have a sense of humor. Indeed, if you are just making jokes all the time, I doubt whether your humor will have the desired effect. Others may not take you seriously.

However, you don't want to be a pompous ass either. If you can show you are human by a mild joke, it will make those who report to you feel more relaxed and comfortable in their dealings with you. This is especially true in times of great stress. A joke doesn't have to be very funny to lessen the strain under these conditions. As General Eisenhower tells us, a sense of humor is a part of leadership.

However, as General Newman cautions us, don't overwork your joking, stay away from crude, off-color, sexist, or racist jokes. Be very careful about joking at others' expense. Far better, as General Smith suggests to tell a joke on yourself. And Field Marshal Wavell shows us, it doesn't take much humor to take our mind off our problems.

The wisdom of the generals tells us:

* Displaying a sense of humor shows others that we are human, especially if we are in charge.

* We don't need to be cracking jokes all the time as we may not be taken seriously.

* Never tell crude, off-color, sexist, or racist jokes.

* Jokes on yourself are better than jokes about others.

IMAGINATION

The most indispensable attribute of the great captain is imagination.
GENERAL OF THE ARMY DOUGLAS MACARTHUR, U.S. Army

There is no victory except through our imaginations.
GENERAL OF THE ARMY DWIGHT D. EISENHOWER, U.S. Army

The development of the power of imagination and its various ramifications is an essential part of general staff training, and an indispensable requisite for leaders of large forces distributed over a considerable area.
GENERAL DER INFANTRIE HUGO BARON VON FREYTAG-LORINGHOVEN,
German Army

Originality, not conventionality, is one of the main pillars of generalship.
MAJOR GENERAL J.F.C. FULLER, British Army

The impossible can only be overborne by the unprecedented.
GENERAL SIR IAN HAMILTON, British Army

Imagination is an extremely important attribute whether for ourselves, for leading organizations, or when serving on a staff. Every victory begins in the mind. We win in the mind before we win in reality.

The psychologist, Dr. Charles Garfield investigated an important technique called mental rehearsal taught to him by Soviet high performance experts as a result of their experiments. In this technique, the subject imagines successful accomplishment of a feat or task repeatedly while in a state of complete and total relaxation. Using this technique, Dr. Garfield himself was able to increase the maximum weight he was able to bench press in a weight lift from 300 to 365 pounds, all in a few hours and in a single evening.

That Garfield was able to learn this technique and apply it proves that the imagination can be developed as General von Freytag-Loringhoven suggests is necessary.

However, the imagination isn't only indispensable to reach our goals, but also in the way these goals are achieved. As General Fuller says, it is originality for which the general should strive. Everyone needs originality, with the imagination being the vehicle for attaining it. For example, conventional wisdom in the film industry was that no actor could succeed without an easily pronounced, Anglo-Saxon name. So most actors fell into line.

Along came Arnold Schwarzenegger. Hollywood pros tried to convince him to change his name. The name "Arnold Strong" was suggested. He laughed and said he would stick to the name he was born with. The experts were horrified. They predicted failure, regardless of his previous bodybuilding success or any acting talents he had or could be developed. Schwarzenegger, indeed! Why people couldn't even pronounce the name. But Arnold stuck to his guns, and today not only is the name Schwarzenegger well known, it is one of the highest paid names in Hollywood. Arnold gives full credit to the originality of his name in getting people to remember it.

Many generals we have quoted noted earlier that "the impossible" could in fact be achieved. General Hamilton tells us how: through the unprecedented. The unprecedented, of course, comes primarily from the imagination.

The wisdom of the generals about imagination is:

★ Imagination is a quality that you can't afford to do without.

★ Your imagination can be developed.

★ Imagination will help you to accomplish the impossible.

INITIATIVE

During war the ball is always kicking around loose in the middle of the field and any man who has the will may pick it up and run with it.

BRIGADIER GENERAL S.L.A. MARSHALL, U.S. Army

If the enemy leaves a door open, you must rush in.

SUN TZU, Ancient Chinese General

I have never given a damn what the enemy was going to do or where he was. What I have known is what I intended to do and then have done it.

GENERAL GEORGE S. PATTON, U.S. Army

It is better to struggle with a stallion when the problem is how to hold it back, than to urge on a bull which refuses to budge.

LIEUTENANT GENERAL MOSHE DAYAN, Army of Israel

The Field Service Regulations require "every officer, under all conditions, to exercise initiative to the maximum extent, without fear of the consequences. Commanding officers must encourage and require this."

GENERAL DER INFANTRIE HUGO BARON VON FREYTAG-LORINGHOVEN,
German Army

Initiative means to be proactive. It means to take the first step. When you're playing in the big leagues, you can't afford to sit around and dawdle. As General Marshall tells us, in life the ball is always kicking around loose in the middle of the field waiting for any individual to pick it up and run with it.

Sometimes your competitor leaves you an opening to fill, and a customer waiting to be satisfied. Don't waste time. The door is open. Rush in!

General Patton is speaking for emphasis when he says he doesn't care about the enemy's intentions. Of course he wants to know them to formulate his strategy. What he is saying is that he's not going to worry about the other fellow; the competition is going to worry about him. This is done by picking up the ball that is rolling around in the middle of the field. It is done by seeing what the enemy intends, that he has left the door open, and by immediately rushing in.

That's why Moshe Dayan is less concerned with subordinates who are charging on ahead and therefore are a little more difficult to control. And it is why General Freytag-Loringhoven says no one who shows initiative should be punished for exceeding their authority.

About initiative, the wisdom of the generals is:

* ⋆ Whatever the situation, "grab the ball and run"—be proactive.
* ⋆ Don't worry about your competitor—show initiative and let him or her worry about you.
* ⋆ Encourage initiative in subordinates, don't punish it.

INTEGRITY

Of all the qualities a leader must have, integrity is the most important.

MAJOR GENERAL PERRY M. SMITH, U.S. Air Force

Of the many attributes necessary for success two are vital—hard work and absolute integrity.

FIELD MARSHAL BERNARD L. MONTGOMERY, British Army

Nothing destroys effectiveness any faster than a lack of integrity or a lack of confidence.

GENERAL RONALD R. FOGLEMAN, U.S. Air Force

War must be carried on systematically, and to do it you must have men of character activated by principles of honor.

GENERAL GEORGE WASHINGTON, Continental Army

Let danger never turn you aside from the pursuit of honor or the service of your country . . . know that death is inevitable and the fame of virtue is immortal.

GENERAL ROBERT E. LEE, Confederate States Army

I n the 1990s, I conducted research into combat leadership applied to non-combat pursuits. I surveyed more than 200 combat leaders, including sixty-two generals and admirals, who went on to very successful civilian careers.[1] Though I expected an encyclopedia of combat leadership concepts applicable to the civilian world, ninety-five percent of the responses I received fell into only eight categories. Their order however, didn't show any particular significance except for only one of the eight categories. In fact, a number wrote short notes or long letters expressing their idea about this one principle. It was clearly first in their minds and many felt it was the basis of all leadership. That principle was integrity.

---

[1] This research was published as *The Stuff of Heroes: The Eight Universal Laws of Leadership* (Longstreet Press, 1998).

What is integrity? In my mind, it is doing what is right, even if no one is watching. General Perry Smith tells the story of Olympic Gold Medal winner Babe Zacharias, who later became a professional golfer. At a major tournament, Zacharias penalized herself two strokes, costing her the tournament. She did this because she said she had accidentally played the wrong ball.

A friend asked, "But Babe . . . why did you do this? No one saw you. No one would have known." "I would have known," answered Babe Zacharias. That's integrity.

In my list of quotations General Perry Smith, whose story about resigning from CNN I've told elsewhere in this book, leads off. He echoes the results of my research. Regarding success, Field Marshal Montgomery concurs in his contribution.

General Fogleman's strong belief in integrity played a major role in his decision not to seek the position of Chairman of the Joint Chiefs of Staff and to leave his position as Chief of Staff of the Air Force a year earlier than required by law. He states that nothing destroys effectiveness more than the lack of integrity.

Why is this? It gets back to our discussion and the wisdom of the generals about trust. People do not follow a leader that they do not trust. If he or she has direct power over them, they do as ordered, but they will rarely put, "life liberty, and sacred honor" on the line for a leader who lacks integrity.

Here again, we see how honor and integrity are bound together. No less an individual than George Washington states that we must have people of character activated by principles of honor. Robert E. Lee admonishes us to not let danger, or anything else deter us in the pursuit of honor, reminding us that death is inevitable, but the fame of virtue (integrity), immortal.

Here, then is the wisdom of the generals about integrity:

* Integrity means doing the right thing, even when no one is looking.

* Integrity is the foundation of all leadership.

* Integrity is the foundation for success.

* A lack of integrity will destroy the effectiveness of any organization.

* Every organization needs people of integrity.

* Death is inevitable, success may be fleeting, but integrity is immortal.

JUDGMENT

There are some roads not to follow; some troops not to strike; some cities not to assault; and some ground which should not be contested.

SUN TZU, Ancient Chinese General

If I am to be hanged for it, I cannot accuse a man who I believe has meant well, and whose error was one of judgment and not of intention.

FIELD MARSHAL ARTHUR WELLESLEY, The Duke of Wellington, British Army

I learned that good judgment comes from experience and that experience grows out of mistakes.

GENERAL OF THE ARMY OMAR N. BRADLEY, U.S. Army

During an operation decisions have usually to be made at once; there may be no time to review the situation or even to think it through. . . . If the mind is to emerge unscathed from this relentless struggle with the unforeseen, two qualities are indispensable: first, an intellect that, even in the darkest hour, retains some glimmerings of the inner light which leads to truth; and second, the courage to follow this faint light wherever it may lead.

MAJOR GENERAL KARL VON CLASEWITZ, Prussian Army

What you have to do is to weigh all the various factors, recognizing that in war half your information may be wrong, that a lot of it is missing completely, and that there are all sorts of elements over which you have no control . . . You have got to weigh all these things and come to a decision as to what you want to do.

FIELD MARSHAL SIR WILLIAM SLIM, British Army

It is too bad we are not all born with good judgment, but this is not the case. The fact is, none of us are. Good judgment must be developed, and the sooner the better, for there is no question that some decisions are much more likely to bring us success than others. That's what Sun Tzu tells us. Sure, there is always an element of luck, but you tend to be luckier when you make good decisions.

Now because we aren't born with good judgment and because no one's judgment is going to be perfect all the time, you've got to factor in good intentions when things go awry due to the poor judgment made by subordinates. General Bradley says this is partly because good judgment is the result of experience, and experience comes from mistakes. We can learn as much or more from our failures as from our successes.

General Clausewitz tells us just how difficult it is to make decisions under extraordinary stress and suggests that the two most useful qualities are a mind which functions at some minimum level of efficiency and the courage to implement its judgment. Field Marshal Slim elaborates on these difficulties, telling us that a lot of our information will be wrong, some missing, and elements present over which we have little control. Still we have to exercise a judgment which leads to success. Sometimes we can do this, sometimes not.

I became very interested in the character of General George Armstrong Custer of Little Big Horn fame several years ago. I was amazed to discover that he was probably the most successful and brilliant cavalry commander of the Civil War, a brigadier general at the tender age of 23 and a major general two years later. His reputation today is that of a crazed commander who due to his ego, got himself and his entire command annihilated. Yet the Battle of Little Big Horn, which he lost, was his only major defeat.

A few years ago, Frederick J. Chiaventone, a former Army officer and instructor at the Army's Command and General Staff College, wrote a fictionalized account of the battle (*A Road We Do Not Know*: Simon and Schuster, 1996). In an author's note, Chiaventone wrote the following:

"A few years ago, while teaching at the Army's Command and General Staff College, I was fortunate enough to be afforded a chance to revisit the site of the battle along with a number of senior military officers for a more in-depth look at the campaign. The colonels and generals on this Staff Ride, all veterans of Vietnam or the Gulf War, were given only that information which was available to Custer and his officers on 25 June 1876 and asked to explain what they would have done in Custer's place. Much to my surprise, and theirs, all of these combat veterans made precisely the same tactical decisions as had the ill-fated commander of the Seventh Cavalry."

Exercising judgment that leads to success is not easy, even for an experienced commander.

The wisdom of the generals lessons on judgment:

* Judgment is important as some decisions are much more likely to lead to success than others.

* Judgment can be developed, but this only comes through experience, and experience, in turn, from mistakes.

* Consider intent in passing judgment on others' decisions.

* Prepare to exercise judgment under very poor conditions with incorrect and incomplete information and elements over which you have little control.

* Sometimes even experienced leaders of proven judgment will make gross errors under the rotten conditions and lack of information with which they are confronted.

JUSTICE

No Connections, Interests, or Intercessions . . . will avail to prevent strict execution of justice.
GENERAL GEORGE WASHINGTON, Continental Army

He [the general] should punish without mercy, especially those who are dearest to him, but never from anger.
FIELD MARSHAL MAURICE COMTE DE SAXE, French Army

A man has justice if he acknowledges the interests of all concerned in any particular transaction rather than serving his own particular interests.
BRIGADIER GENERAL S.L.A. MARSHALL, U.S. Army

As an officer rises higher in his profession, the demands made upon him in the administration of justice increase.
GENERAL SIR JOHN W. HACKETT, British Army

It is utterly stupid to say that general officers, as a result of whose orders thousands of gallant and brave men have been killed, are not capable of knowing how to remove the life of one miserable poltroon.
GENERAL GEORGE S. PATTON, JR., U.S. Army

If we are to be given responsibility for others in any situation, we must strive to be just. This doesn't mean that we bend over so far backward to be fair to others that we treat our friends unfairly. However, it does mean that our friends or those who in other ways have special relationships with us receive no better and no worse treatment than anyone else. That is justice.

How can we best do this? General Marshall explains it: acknowledge the interests of all concerned rather than serving our own particular interests, whatever they may be.

The higher you rise in life, the more demands will be placed on you in this regard. In many organizations, your very advancement is based on what others have thought about your administration of justice, formal or informal, at different levels of responsibility. However, even if you are not a member of a formal organization, a rise in your profession means greater influence. A psychologist, attorney, or professor becomes better known and thus more influential. Your opinions count more, and what you say and do will count more and more and you will have more and more opportunities to demonstrate justice . . . or injustice.

This is as it should be. You have increased responsibility for justice, and as Patton explains, this power is not misplaced. It is the natural result of your achievements. It is up to you to guard against its misuse.

The wisdom of the generals about justice:

* You administer justice fairly by acknowledging the interests of all parties rather than serving your own.

* As you rise in your profession, you will have increasing responsibility to ensure that justice is served.

* This power is not misplaced—it is up to you to ensure it is not misused.

LEADERSHIP

The relations between officers and enlisted men should in no sense be that of superior and inferior, nor of that of master and servant, but rather that of teacher and scholar.

LIEUTENANT GENERAL JOHN A. LEJEUNE, U.S. Marine Corps

The principles of leadership in the military are the same as they are in business, in the church, and elsewhere: a. Learn your job. (This involves study and hard work.) b. Work hard at your job. C. Train your people. D. Inspect frequently to see that the job is being done properly.

ADMIRAL HYMAN G. RICKOVER, U.S. Navy

An army of stags led by a lion is more to be feared than an army of lions led by a stag.

PHILIP OF MACEDONIA, Ancient Macedonian Ruler

A competent leader can get efficient service from poor troops, while on the contrary an incapable leader can demoralize the best of troops.

GENERAL OF THE ARMIES JOHN J. PERSHING, U.S. Army

I don't think you have to be wearing stars on your shoulders or have "commander" in your title to be a leader. Anybody who wants to raise his hand can be a leader any time.

GENERAL RONALD R. FOGLEMAN, U.S. Air Force

Leadership is not manipulation or a trick of management. It is a trust. Many have the entirely wrong idea about leadership. For them, it's some kind of power trip. So their idea of leadership is ordering everyone around. I'm not saying that the military doesn't have people like this. But, we try to get rid of them as soon as possible. Re-read what General Lejeune said about the relationship between the leader and those led. He was once Commandant of the Marine Corps and he knew.

As Admiral Rickover clearly shows, the principles are the same no matter our line of work. If you drop a pencil, it always falls down, not sideways or up. Yet, there are many definitions of leadership. Mine is this: to help others to perform at the their highest level of productivity in accomplishing any task or reaching any goal.

Some say we don't need leaders today. We just sort of get together and do things . . . like ants someone told me. I rather doubt it. Ants do a lot, but they do not reason. They do not worry. They do not feel the pangs of failure. They do not exult in success. Men and women do. So, leadership is the decisive factor in much of what we do.

As Philip of Macedonia and General Pershing agree, outstanding organizations can be driven into the ground by incompetent leadership and mediocre or worse organizations made great by great leaders.

If you remember the old series "Baa Baa Black Sheep" on TV some years ago, you saw the amazing story of the 214th Fighter Squadron of the U.S. Marine Corps, the highest scoring day fighter squadron in the Pacific Theater. This squadron was commanded by Major (later Colonel) Pappy Boyington who also created the squadron. Sine they were so good, you'd think they were made up of the Marine Corps finest fighter pilots. They may have been . . . afterwards, but the 214th was originally a temporary squadron. It was Boyington's idea. The squadron was formed of misfits and outcasts from other squadrons. Some were even awaiting trial for court-martial offenses. But Boyington turned them into the best.

However, the really interesting thing about leadership to me is that you do not have to be a manager or supervisor to be a leader. As General Fogelman states all you need to do is raise your hand and volunteer. There are many openings for leaders in any organization, from running the Savings Bond Drive to organizing the Holiday Party. All require leaders.

Interestingly, many refuse these jobs. "Promote me to be a manager, and then I'll be a leader," they say. They don't understand that this is like Aesop's tale of the man who told the stove that he would give it wood if first the stove would give him heat. It doesn't work that way. You need to demonstrate leadership first, then you'll be promoted.

What does the wisdom of the generals say about leadership?

* ★ Leadership isn't manipulation or a power trip—it is a trust.
* ★ The principles of leadership are universal to all organizations.
* ★ Leadership spells the difference between effective and ineffective organizations.
* ★ You don't need to be a manager or supervisor to be a leader—all you need to do is raise your hand.

LEARNING

War is not an affair of chance. A great deal of knowledge, study, and meditation is necessary to conduct it well.

FREDERICK THE GREAT, German Emperor

Even the largest-scale peace maneuvers are only a feeble shadow of the real thing. So that a soldier desirous of acquiring skill in handling troops is forced to theoretical study of Great Captains.

FIELD MARSHAL ARCHIBALD P. WAVELL, British Army

We should never pretend to know what we don't know, we should not feel ashamed to ask and learn from people below, and we should listen carefully to the views of the cadres at the lowest levels. Be a pupil before you become a teacher; learn from the cadres at the lower levels before you issue orders.

MAO TSE-TUNG, Chinese Revolutionary Leader

A liberally educated person meets new ideas with curiosity and fascination. An illiberally educated person meets new ideas with fear.

VICE ADMIRAL JAMES B. STOCKDALE, U.S. Navy

Officers, particularly those in positions of command, must at all times be urged to expand the scope of their knowledge; nothing has a more damaging effect on the quality of the army than a hard core of commanders whose minds are narrow and inflexible.

MAJOR GENERAL YIGAEL ALLON, Army of Israel

Frederick the Great tells us that war is not based on chance. Therefore knowledge, study, and meditation are required. Many, if not most, of the activities in life are in this category, from games like chess, poker, and backgammon, to professions such as business, medicine, or law. Sure, chance is a factor in all of these endeavors. However, it is learning that spells the difference between competence and incompetence and between success and failure.

Because war is concerned with the leadership, management, and utilization of human beings in life and death situations, it is not inaccurate to say that those who fail to learn through prior study when they can do so are little short of murderers. But many other professions likewise punish others through the incompetence of the professional. The client defended by the incompetent attorney may be imprisoned or executed. The patient treated by an incompetent physician may lose his health. Workers employed by an incompetent businessman may lose their livelihood; customers their savings. The result of lack of learning by the professional can always be catastrophic to both the practitioner and to those that work with him or depend on him for results. So, Field Marshal Wavell is on target when he recommends theoretical study of war. This is true of all professions, since no one lives so long that he or she alone, can attain the required experience.

Mao Tse-tung cautions never to pretend to know what we do not, and urges us to listen to others and not be afraid to learn from those who we would teach. Most teachers will tell you that they learn at least as much from their students as from their own studies.

Finally, both Admiral Stockdale and General Yadin introduce the concept of continuous learning in different ways. Learning as a professional is a lifetime occupation. This is not only because the reservoir of knowledge in each of our professions is so great although it is. But more than that, required knowledge is constantly expanding and requires our attention. When I wrote my doctoral dissertation a little over twenty years ago, I did so on a typewriter. Today, typewriters barely exist, and anyone who completed a dissertation, with all the revisions, corrections, etc. necessary on a typewriter would probably be viewed as quite eccentric. Fifteen years ago, I surveyed senior executives asking if they use a computer at work. Most answered something to the effect that people who worked for them did. I know of few senior executives today who do not have a computer close by for their personal use.

A few years ago, the internet did not exist. Even five years ago, few companies were making money through marketing over the internet or the worldwide web. Today, e-commerce sales are in the billions. Many businesses and professions have been changed dramatically because of it, even if they don't use it to sell a product directly.

About learning, the wisdom of the generals tells us:

* What we do is not based on chance; therefore learning continually makes the difference between success and failure.

* The professional incompetent for lack of learning is a criminal.

* Do not be afraid to learn from those who report to you.

* Learning is a required lifetime commitment.

LOGISTICS

Logistics comprises the means and arrangements which work out the plans of strategy and tactics. Strategy decides where to act; logistics brings the troops to this point.

GENERAL HENRI DE JOMINI, French Army, Russian Army

The more I see of war, the more I realize how it all depends on administration and transportation . . . It takes little skill or imagination to see where you would like your forces to be and when; it takes much knowledge and hard work to know where you can place your forces and whether you can maintain them there.

FIELD MARSHAL EARL WAVELL, British Army

Nine times out of ten an army has been destroyed because its supply lines have been severed.

GENERAL OF THE ARMY DOUGLAS MACARTHUR, U.S. Army

Communications dominate war; broadly considered, they are the most important single element in strategy, political or military.

REAR ADMIRAL ALFRED THAYER MAHAN, U.S. Navy

The whole secret of the art of war lies in the ability to become master of the lines of communication.

NAPOLEON BONAPARTE, French Emperor

It is one thing to decide on a prefect strategy. If you cannot implement that strategy due to the inadequacy of your logistics, than you better find some other strategy. Logistics has to do with the implementation and execution of your plans. It is so important, that frequently battles are decided solely on this factor. In business, logistics has to do with the how, when and where of distributing your product or service and getting it to your customer.

For example, what good is your unique product if your distributor does not get it to your customer? It doesn't make any difference if you have the perfect product for winter use in Afghanistan if available transportation can't get it there until spring. Who cares if your product is lowest in price if it is unavailable where and when your customer can buy it?

This is like the old joke of the customer going to buy a certain stereo system. She goes to the store and asks the storeowner the price. "This system is $500," he says. "Why that's outrageous," the woman responds. "Your competitor across the street sells the exact same system for only $400!" "In that case, why don't you buy it from him?" asks the owner. "I would," says the woman, "but he is out of stock now." "Well," says the owner, "when we're out of stock we sell this system for $400, too."

Less amusing is when one of my publishers failed to distribute one of my books to the bookstores in sufficient time before Christmas several years ago. It may have been a great book (I thought it was) but our sales certainly didn't meet expectations because of this logistical failure.

The true problem with logistics is that we tend to give it short shrift. We spend millions in resources developing wonderful products and services, constructing wonderful plans and strategies, executing great advertising campaigns and sales promotions. Then, we blow it all by assuming logistics will take care of themselves.

Yet, as the wisdom of the generals tell us:

★ Logistics dominate other aspects of your operations.

★ Operational failures usually boil down to a failure in logistics.

★ Master logistics and you master one of the great secrets of business success.

LUCK

Luck in the long run is given only to the efficient.

FIELD MARSHAL COUNT HELMUTH VON MOLKE, German Army

Most army officers who grumble about the luck of their more favored brothers either are not honest with themselves or they have not taken the pains to analyze the reasons for the success of their more fortunate fellow officers.

GENERAL OF THE AIR FORCE HENRY H. ARNOLD, U.S. Air Force

When a general conducts himself with all prudence, he still can suffer ill fortune; for how many things oppose his labors! Weather, harvest, his officers, the health of his troops, blunders, the death of an officer on whom he counts, discouragement of the troops, exposure of his spies, negligence of the officers who should reconnoiter the enemy and, finally, betrayal. These are the things that should be kept continually before your eyes so as to be prepared for them and prevent good fortune from blinding us.

FREDERICK THE GREAT, German Emperor

I base my calculation on the expectation that luck will be against me.

NAPOLEON BONAPARTE, French Emperor

Fortune or fate decides one half our life; the other half depends on ourselves.

FIELD MARSHAL BERNARD L. MONTGOMERY, British Army

The wisdom of the generals is not that luck doesn't exist, but that basically we control our destiny and the outcome of our endeavors ourselves. That is the gist of Field Marshal von Molke's conclusion that in the long run, luck comes only to the efficient. Rather than attributing failure to achieve the desired results to luck, General Arnold recommends an introspection and an analysis of others success.

This is somewhat in tune with motivational coach Tony Robbins' assertion. Robbins is the fellow that got President Clinton to do a firewalk at Camp David. Robbins says that success leaves clues. Therefore, if you want the same success, analyze what others have done and do the same. He agrees with Arnold that success isn't just luck.

The insights provided by Emperors Frederick and Napoleon go together. Frederick says an awful lot of things can go wrong and that you have to foresee them and make allowances for them ahead of time. When they occur, it's not just bad luck . . . that's the norm. Napoleon takes it once step further. He says to assume that things will go wrong; that you will have bad luck. Then, make your plans accordingly.

Finally we have Field Marshal Montgomery who calculates that one half of what happens we have no control over. It's just luck or fate. However, we do have control over the other half.

Regarding luck, the generals say:

* ★ Become more efficient; you'll find yourself luckier.
* ★ Analyze those you consider lucky and model their achievements.
* ★ Bad luck will occur, so plan and allow for it.
* ★ Fate may control one half of what happens, but you control the other half.

MISTAKES

When a man has committed no faults in war, he can only have been engaged in it but a short time.

MARSHAL OF FRANCE VICOMTE DE TURENNE, French Army

War is replete with mistakes because it is full of improvisations.

ADMIRAL HYMAN G. RICKOVER, U.S. Navy

It is always a bad sign in an army when scapegoats are habitually sought out and brought to sacrifice for every conceivable mistake.

FIELD MARSHAL ERWIN ROMMEL, German Army

You must be able to underwrite the honest mistakes of your subordinates if you wish to develop their initiative and experience

GENERAL BRUCE C. CLARKE, U.S. Army

If you ever make any mistakes, be quick to admit and especially to correct them. While this manner of conducting oneself is totally natural and is not deserving of praise, it will however draw praise for you, and win you hearts and will allow you to pardon mistakes in others.

MARSHAL DE BELLE-ISLE, French Army

Mistakes are going to happen. You and I have made them in the past and unfortunately, we're going to make them again in the future. If you haven't made any mistakes in your work, you've either not been at it for a very long time, or you're not doing very much.

At any job where improvisation is required, and that includes everything from ditch-digging to acting to dog-training, you are at times going to have to improvise. If you're good, many of those improvisations will work. But no matter how good you are, sometimes they will not. Admiral Rickover who built the world's first nuclear submarine, and was the architect of our nuclear navy knew this only too well.

If you are running the show and you are some kind of zero-defects freak and feel compelled to punish every mistake, you are discouraging innovation, risk-taking and many other desirable actions. Years ago at IBM, a new vice president screwed up and lost a million dollars in one of his first projects. Feeling disgraced, he was called in by IBM founder Thomas Watson. "I guess you want to fire me," said the young vice president. "Fire you!" exclaimed Watson. "We just invested a million dollars as part of your education." As both Field Marshal Rommel of the German Army and General Bruce Clarke, of the American Army agree. You've got to be able to underwrite the mistakes of those who work for you so as to develop and "educate" them.

When you make a mistake, own up to it. Don't try to cover it up and pretend it never happened and wasn't really a mistake at all. And for goodness sake, don't ever blame it on someone else, especially not someone that works for you. You will deservedly lose the respect of your bosses, your employees and your associates.

The wisdom of the generals regarding mistakes is:

* Mistakes are going to happen.
* The more and harder you work, the more challenging your job, the more mistakes you are likely to make.
* Use the mistakes of those that report to you to develop their talents and abilities.
* When you make a mistake, own up to it and take full responsibility.

MORALE

Morale is the state of mind. It is the steadfastness and courage and hope. It is confidence and zeal and loyalty. It is staying power, the spirit which endures to the end—the will to win. With it all things are possible, without it everything else, planning, preparation, production count for naught.

GENERAL GEORGE C. MARSHAL, U.S. Army

Morale is the greatest single factor in successful war.

GENERAL DWIGHT D. EISENHOWER, U.S. Army

The capability of an individual and the capability of a ship can be enhanced by some 20 to 30 percent if morale is high.

ADMIRAL ELMO R. ZUMWALT, JR., U.S. Navy

No system of tactics can lead to victory when the morale of an army is bad.

GENERAL HENRI DE JOMINI, Russian Army

The oldest method for manufacturing high morale is to convince the soldier, and the officer as well, that he is a member of the best organization of its kind in the military service.

GENERAL OF THE AIR FORCE HENRY H. ARNOLD, U.S. Air Force

As General Marshal tells us, morale is a state of mind. It's the mental and emotional feeling an individual has regarding what is expected of him. With it, all things are possible. General Eisenhower calls it the greatest single factor for success in war. Admiral Zumwalt calculates that with it individual capacity and the capability of a ship may be increased by 20 to 30 percent. General Jomini gives us the down side. He says that nothing is going to lead us to victory when morale is bad.

From all of this, we gather that we have hit on one of those elements which can easily be the difference between success and failure in our organizations. Now the only problem is how to develop it? General

Arnold tells us that the oldest method is to convince the individual that he is a member of the best organization of its type in the world. Great! How do we do that? I found the following three ways work pretty well. First, celebrate, recognize, and promote every individual and organizational success. That way everyone can appreciate and share in the accomplishments. Find ways to build ownership such as inviting others to participate in decision-making as much as practical. Ownership makes it "our" company rather than "theirs." Finally, know what's going on in your organization by personal observation so that you can fix the problems and take advantage of the opportunities. You can't learn all this by sitting in your office. Get out where others can see you and what you are about. Get out to make sure your messages are getting to those who must execute them and so that you can understand and help solve the real problems on the firing line.

According to the wisdom of the generals:

★ Morale is a state of mind and emotional feeling.

★ High morale will help you to win; with low morale you are likely to lose.

★ The best way of building high morale is by convincing your soldiers or employees that they are in the best organization of its type in the world.

MOTIVATION

A soldier doesn't fight very hard for someone who is going to shoot him on a whim. That's not what leadership is about.

GENERAL H. NORMAN SCHWARZKOPF, U.S. Army

A man does not have himself killed for a half-pence a day or for a petty distinction. You must speak to the soul in order to excite him.

NAPOLEON BONAPARTE, Emperor of France

*A*lso worth remembering is that in any man's dark hour, a pat on the back and an earnest handclasp may well work a small miracle.

BRIGADIER GENERAL S.L.A. MARSHALL, U.S. Army

*B*ecause a good general regards his men as sons, they will march with him into the deepest valleys. He treats them as his own beloved sons and they will die with him.

SUN TZU, Ancient Chinese General

*M*en who think that their officer recognizes them are keener to be seen doing something honorable and more desirous of avoiding disgrace.

XENOPHON, Ancient Greek General

There are many ways of motivating others towards worthwhile goals, and in this section our contributors speak to a variety of them. General Schwarzkopf points out that while a military leader has the power to enforce obedience, this, in itself, is usually a very poor motivator. In fact, if you routinely use the power of the gun, what are your soldiers likely to do the first chance they feel they can get away with it? Run away, of course! If your organization has a large turnover because folks keep quitting, you better give some thought to this.

Napoleon opens an interesting issue. Will others routinely risk their lives day in and day out for money? Yes, people do risk their lives for high sums of money. Various types of sports car racing and boxing come to mind. However, these are events of risk and are somewhat co-mingled with what we might call "love of the sport."

Research over the last fifty years has repeatedly demonstrated that once basic monetary and security needs are satisfied, respect, interesting work, recognition and a chance to develop one's skills are far more important.

This, by the way, calls into question the so-called "all volunteer army" which we have had in the U.S. for the last thirty years or so. The idea is to attract individuals by paying whatever they are worth. Forget the traditional ideas of duty, honor, and patriotism. We treat military service like any other job and pay whatever it takes to get the people we need. We don't even encourage them to wear their uniforms when they are off duty.

Without a long-term shooting war, we have been able to get by with this concept, although personnel costs have increased astronomically. However, currently all military services are having a lot of trouble. The economy is pretty good, so the cost to attract the high quality folks intelligent and educated enough to use today's complex weapons systems gets higher and higher. At the same time, what is called the "ops tempo" or intensity of operations is getting pretty severe. For example, those who are on aircrew duties in one of the services may be away from home and flying combat over Kosovo, Iraq, or somewhere else as much as six months out of the year.

Now, since under the all-volunteer army concept military service is only a job like any other job, flying with an airline with a much reduced workload, little risk, and to make more than a general makes in about three years is an extremely attractive alternative. Not only are all the services having difficulty retaining pilots, but they are paying big monetary bonuses to pilots who agree to stay a few more years. This, in turn, causes additional morale problems for those who suffer the same risks in flying and have the same family problems due to the ops temp and do not get the big bonuses because they are not pilots.

With this incredible situation existing, I sometimes marvel that our military leaders are able to motivate their younger troops at all. They do despite the problem with "the system" as presently constituted. They follow Sun Tzu's recommendation and treat their subordinates as they would their own beloved sons and daughters. As a result their soldiers are ready to go all the way with them.

This is the wisdom of the generals regarding motivation:

* ⋆ Don't use your power as a routine motivator.

* ⋆ There is a lot more that motivates besides security, high pay, or benefits.

* ⋆ Respect, interesting work, recognition, and a chance to develop one's skills can be your most important motivators.

* ⋆ Treat your followers as you would your own progeny.

OPPORTUNITY

The important thing is to see the opportunity and know how to use it.

FIELD MARSHAL MAURICE COMTE DE SAXE, French Army

Learn to profit from local circumstances.

FIELD MARSHAL ALEKSANDR V. SUVOROV, Russian Army

To our men . . . the jungle was a strange fearsome place; moving and fighting in it were a nightmare . . . To us it appeared only as an obstacle to movement; to the Japanese it was a welcome means of concealed maneuver and surprise . . . The Japanese reaped the deserved reward . . . we paid the penalty.

FIELD MARSHAL VISCOUNT SLIM, British Army

Thus, those skilled at making the enemy move do so by creating a situation to which he must conform; they entice him with something he is certain to take, and with lures of ostensible profit they await him in strength. Therefore, a skilled commander seeks victory from the situation and does not demand it of his subordinates.

SUN TZU, Ancient Chinese General

Not only strike when the iron is hot, but make it hot by striking.

OLIVER CROMWELL, English Army

Opportunities are all around us, if we will but see them. Many individuals have discovered that in every problem lies the seed of an equal or even greater benefit. How can this be? I don't know, but it is true. In Los Angeles, Nicole Dionne had a great idea on how to greatly increase sales in the production of sounds. Yes, businesses really pay for manufactured sounds. In this case, Hollywood studios. She even went to the trouble of developing a marketing plan showing exactly how to do this. Her company wouldn't buy it. So Nicole quit and started her own successful sound company called Primeval Scream.

David Overton had studied music, but his parents were in failing health and needed him to help run their restaurant. He knew little about the business, but he loved cheesecakes. So, he saved their business by doing it his way. He built the famous Cheesecake Factory chain of restaurants into a several hundred million-dollar operation with 50 plus restaurants as of this writing and more opening all the time.

My friend Joe Cossman, who made millions of dollars selling ant farms, potato guns, imitation shrunken human heads to hang on automobile rear-view mirrors and other off-beat products tells me its all in how you look at things. This former World War II soldier agrees with Field Marshal Slim. He told me once how a man brought a failed product to him once consisting of earrings with little bells on each. He saw the same product differently. He called them "mother-in-law" earrings—with the bells to warn of her approach—and sold a small fortune's worth.

One man's jungle nightmare is another's source of concealment, surprise and advantage. It's all how you look at the situation. To put it in Field Marshal Surovov's words, we must learn to profit from local circumstances. Both Sun Tzu and Cromwell agree that we can create opportunity from the situation ourselves.

Here, then, is the wisdom of the generals regarding opportunity:

* Opportunities are all around us wherever we are located and whatever industry we are in.

* The trick is how we look at things—in every problem lies an opportunity of equal or greater benefit.

* We create our own opportunities ourselves.

OPTIMISM

Optimism and pessimism are infectious and they spread more rapidly from the head downward than in any other direction. . . . I firmly determined that my mannerisms and speech in public would always reflect the cheerful certainty of victory—that any pessimism and discouragement I might ever feel would be reserved for my pillow.

GENERAL OF THE ARMY DWIGHT D. EISENHOWER, U.S. Army

Perpetual optimism is a force multiplier.

GENERAL COLIN POWELL, U.S. Army

A pragmatically optimistic individual who is not a Pollyanna, but who comes to work with a lot of enthusiasm and optimism, tends to be an effective and respected leader. Although a cynic might do a good job as a leader, this cynicism and pessimism may soon transfer negatively throughout the organization.

MAJOR GENERAL PERRY M. SMITH, U.S. Air Force

I shall expect nothing short of success.

GENERAL PHILIP SHERIDAN, U.S. Army

There's your target and this is your axis of advance. Don't signal me during the fighting for more men, arms or vehicles. All that we could allocate you've already got, and there isn't more. Keep signaling your advances.

LIEUTENANT GENERAL MOSHE DAYAN, Army of Israel

You make think that optimism or pessimism make little difference to an organization or its success, but that is incorrect. The fact is, others take their lead from you. I have found that even if I am not the designated leader on a project or in a situation, that I can positively influence the attitudes of others and even the outcome of work toward a task or goal by being optimistic. Partly I believe this is because as Eisenhower states, optimism is infectious.

Moreover, I don't know about you, but I would prefer to be around someone who is optimistic rather than one who is not. Certainly a leader who is pessimistic about reaching our goals doesn't fill me with any hope that we will be able to do so. As a matter of fact, when the boss says, "I don't think we can do thus and so" in any organization, that word gets around and usually, that prediction turns out to be accurate. Even a grim looking face or a depressed demeanor can cause all sorts of unintended and undesirable results. Your people say, "Uh-oh, the boss is upset something's wrong. We're in trouble." And the word spreads like wildfire with all sorts of bizarre speculation as to what is going on. Better to keep your negative feelings to yourself.

Now, when you appear positive, that word gets around fast too. The word on the grapevine is: "The boss is pleased. Something good must have happened. We must be winning." So everyone goes around acting like winners. That's why success builds on success. No wonder Colin Powell says that optimism causes your force to have several times its normal effect.

As a thirty-four year old senior general during the Civil War, Sheridan really did expect success. Maybe he was a little harsh and overly optimistic at times. He once fired a senior general, not because he didn't perform properly and win, but because he didn't do so fast enough to suit Sheridan. Still Sheridan's role in the final victory was considered second only to Generals Grant and Sherman. General Dayan gives us much the same optimistic perspective when he instructs his subordinate generals: "Keep signaling your advances."

The wisdom of the generals tells us this about optimism:

* ★ Optimism or pessimism is highly infectious, so make it optimism.
* ★ Optimism multiplies the productivity of your organization several times its normal output.
* ★ Optimistic leaders expect positive results—and get them.

PEOPLE

Wars may be fought with weapons, but they are won by men. It is the spirit of the men who follow and of the man who leads that gains the victory.

GENERAL GEORGE S. PATTON, JR., U.S. Army

Historically, good men with poor ships are better than poor men with good ships.

ADMIRAL J.K. TAUSSIG, U.S. Navy

Machines are nothing without men.

ADMIRAL ERNEST J. KING, U.S. Navy

A general's principal talent consists in knowing the mentality of the soldier and in winning his confidence.

NAPOLEON BONAPARTE, French Emperor

Know your men and be constantly on the alert for potential leaders—you never know how soon you may need them.

GENERAL MATTHEW B. RIDGWAY, U.S. Army

People are your most important asset in any organization. That may sound like a bumper sticker, but the generals know it to be true. Patton's statement that it is men, rather than weapons, that win wars, is proven throughout history by countries with inferior weapons who nevertheless manage to win over those who have technological superiority.

The two admirals are saying something very similar . . . it's the people who must do the job that count every time. That's why companies that don't take care of their people or manage and lead them poorly, are in a heap of trouble no matter their financial resources, products, or other positive factors. These companies can lose out to smaller competitors with fewer resources, but that have policies to attract and keep happy employees and take better advantage of their capabilities.

The implications of the importance of people for the organization are several. First, you must get and keep good people. Then, you must train them well and develop their potential. You must continually promote them into positions where their talents can be best utilized and perfected. Finally, you must study them and know them as individuals as well or better than you know and understand any technical discipline or piece of machinery in order to motivate and help them perform to their personal best.

The wisdom of the generals regarding people:

* ☆ People constitute your most important resource.
* ☆ Develop and implement policies to keep good people.
* ☆ Train people and develop their potential.
* ☆ Promote people into positions where their talents can be best utilized and perfected.
* ☆ Know and understand your people so that you can motivate and help them to perform at their personal best.

PERSISTENCE

There must be a beginning of any great matter, but the continuing unto the end until it be thoroughly finished yields the true glory.

ADMIRAL SIR FRANCIS DRAKE, British Navy

We fight, get beat, rise, fight again.

MAJOR GENERAL NATHANAEL GREENE, Continental Army

In case of doubt, push on just a little further and then keep on pushing.

GENERAL GEORGE S. PATTON, JR., U.S. Army

One of my superstitions had always been when I started to go anywhere, or do anything, not to turn back, or stop until the thing intended was accomplished.

GENERAL ULYSSES S. GRANT, U.S. Army

The advantages of the enemy will have but little value if we do not permit them to impair our resolution.

GENERAL ROBERT E. LEE, Confederate States Army

Persistence, the ability to go on despite difficulties, is necessary for the accomplishment of almost any worthwhile goal, because difficulties of one sort or another are practically inevitable. That's why Sir Francis Drake says that the true glory of any endeavor lies in continuing a project until the end.

General Greene represents much of how the war went when we fought our War of Independence against the mighty British Empire, the superpower of the day. We lost more battles than we ever won. In every case, the Continental Army just picked itself up and fought again. However, eventually we prevailed. That's the value of persistence. That's why General Patton says that when in doubt, we should just keep going.

Too many quit along the way before they ever get there. I can't tell you how many times I have met writers who tell me that they wrote a book, but just couldn't get it published. "How many publishers did you try?" I ask. "Oh six or seven . . . a lot," is a typical answer. "Every single one turned me down."

I then tell them my story with my first book. I wrote to thirty-one publishers before I went on contract. That first book sold more than 50,000 copies! I have met authors that were rejected more than that. I'm told that Jack Canfield and Mark Victor Hansen who wrote the "Chicken Soup" series, which has sold millions of copies were turned down by more than sixty publishers. I am constantly reminded that successful people do things that unsuccessful people simply won't do.

This was undoubtedly one of the reasons for Grant's success during the Civil War. I guess for the sake of the country, we can be glad that Grant had such a superstition. Maybe one of the reasons that Lee did so well for so long with inferior resources was that he didn't allow anything to "impair his resolution" despite the great resources of his adversaries.

Regarding persistence, the wisdom of the generals is:

★ If in doubt, keep moving toward your goals.

★ If you run into obstacles, that's normal, keep going.

★ Success may be just one step forward, you never know how close you are.

★ Resolve to persist until you get there.

PLANNING

In war nothing is achieved except by calculation. Everything that is not soundly planned in its details yields no result.

NAPOLEON BONAPARTE, French Emperor

The commander must decide how he will fight the battle before it begins.

FIELD MARSHAL BERNARD L. MONTGOMERY, British Army

Each commander's plan had to be clear so that every other commander would understand what his colleagues were doing—what their objectives were, and how they intended to accomplish them.

MAJOR GENERAL ARIEL SHARON, Army of Israel

No operation plan extends with any certainty beyond the first encounter with the main body of the enemy. . . . Planning is everything. Plans are nothing.

FIELD MARSHAL HELMUTH GRAF VON MOLKE, German Army

A good plan violently executed Now is better than a perfect plan next week.

GENERAL GEORGE S. PATTON, JR., U.S. Army

The generals make it clear that you must plan before you achieve. Why is this? Well, you must establish clear goals and objectives. You can't get "there" until you know where "there" is. An analysis of the situation you face helps you to establish realistic goals and objectives in the situation you face as well as indicating problems to be overcome, threats to be avoided, and opportunities to be taken advantage of. Through the planning process we clearly see our advantages and disadvantages and those of our competitors. We are able to create a strategy and tactics likely to lead to success.

The planning process helps to establish a roadmap which lays out how you will get from where you are now until you reach your objectives and goals. It is no accident that every pilot develops a flight plan for flights outside of a local area, even if he or she has flown a specific route a hundred times or more. Every airline flight, for example, files a flight plan before it is permitted to take off. The idea is to make all the necessary calculations in advance. For the same reason, it is folly to begin any complex operation without planning.

Battles and businesses share this element: both are complex, requiring the integration and utilization of the talents and resources of many different skills, departments, vendors, and suppliers. These must all fit together most efficiently so that each is on time and this timing makes the maximum use of our available people, capital, and equipment. Thus as General Sharon says, we must think this through and put this in our plan.

Field Marshal von Molke tells us that no matter how much our efforts, or how good our plans, they don't survive unmodified very long. Why is that? Because the environment is constantly changing. Much happens that we thought unlikely. Much that we thought likely doesn't happen. Isn't the whole exercise then a big waste of time? No, von Molke explains. Though plans are nothing, planning is everything. Because of the intellectual process we must go through to develop our plans, we have anticipated various alternatives and know what to do when they occur. We have stimulated our thinking to get the best and most efficient use of our limited resources.

Patton gives us some final advice: beware of unnecessary delay. Opportunities in business, battle, and life are always fleeting. A so-so plan executed to the best of your ability today may be better than the finely tuned, perfect plan executed tomorrow.

The wisdom of the generals about planning is:

* ⋆ Plans are necessary for all major endeavors before engagement.
* ⋆ Plans help us see the situation clearly so that we can prepare for success.
* ⋆ Plans may be nothing, but planning is everything.
* ⋆ Never delay awaiting perfection in a plan.

PREPAREDNESS

To be prepared for war is one of the most effectual means of preserving the peace.
GENERAL GEORGE WASHINGTON, Continental Army

If the experience of four wars during my lifetime gives me any license to dispense advice, it is to remember how unprepared we were before each of these conflicts. We should never allow this to happen again.
GENERAL JAMES "JIMMY" DOOLITTLE, U.S. Air Force

You think out every possible development and decide on the way to deal with the situation created. When one of these developments occur; you put your plan in operation, and everyone says, "What genius . . ." whereas the credit is really due to the labor of preparation.
MARSHAL OF FRANCE FERDINAND FOCH, French Army

If I take so many precautions, it is because it is my custom to leave nothing to chance.
NAPOLEON BONAPARTE, Emperor of France

Since "preparedness ensures success and unpreparedness spells failure," there can be no victory in war without advance planning and preparations.
MAO TSE-TUNG, Chinese Revolutionary Leader

Going right along with planning is preparation or preparedness. If we are really prepared, we are ready for anything. Sometimes it seems that when we are prepared, nothing happens. We take an umbrella and it does not rain. We joke and say that we prevented the rain by bringing our umbrella. Sometimes our preparedness is seen by a competitor and prevents him from acting. We obtain the lease of a building to construct a new store in a certain area. As a result, our competitor decides not to construct a similar store. This may occur whether we actually build or not. A bully threatens to beat up a teenager. The teenager learns karate. The bully decides to pick on someone else.

Believe it or not, a few years ago a small town in the southeastern U.S. passed a law that every household had to keep a loaded gun. Contrary to all sorts of dire predictions as to the folly of this ordinance, the crime rate plummeted after this fact became known throughout the county.

There is little question that if we prepare for any event, whether desired or not, we will handle it better. As Field Marshal Foch says, they call it genius, but it was really preparedness.

Leaving nothing to chance, like Napoleon, gives you a leg up on success. Many students who have done poorly on exams have, in fact, studied. However, they ignored certain areas assuming little likelihood of being asked about it, and rushed through other parts on the same theory. They left too much to chance and did not prepare properly. The students that do well invariably study and prepare at a much higher level. Like Napoleon, they leave nothing to chance.

Finally, Mao Tse-tung tells us that without preparedness, there can be no victory. If we want success; if we want to reach our goals, we must prepare. No wonder the Boy Scouts' motto is: Be Prepared!

Here's what the wisdom of the generals tells us about preparedness:

* ☆ If you are truly prepared, you are ready for anything.
* ☆ Preparedness can sometimes forestall the event we want to avoid.
* ☆ When you are prepared, you leave little to chance.
* ☆ Without preparedness there can be no success.

PROBLEM SOLVING

All problems, personal, national, or combat, become smaller if you don't dodge them, but confront them. Touch a thistle timidly and it pricks you; grasp it boldly, and its spines crumble.

ADMIRAL WILLIAM F. HALSEY, U.S. Navy

In war we are always doing something for the first time. It would be a miracle if what we improvised under the stress of war should be perfect.

ADMIRAL HYMAN RICKOVER, U.S. Navy

I must have assistants who will solve their own problems and tell me later what they have done.

GENERAL OF THE ARMY GEORGE C. MARSHALL, U.S. Army

A leader should facilitate problem solving, but should let subordinates solve most problems.

MAJOR GENERAL PERRY M. SMITH, U.S. Air Force

The officer is therefore badly advised who would believe that a hunch is without value.

BRIGADIER GENERAL S.L.A. MARSHALL, U.S. Army

We will be engaged in problem solving for the rest of our lives, so it makes a lot of sense to consider what the generals have learned over the years as to how best to go about it. Admiral Halsey tells us not to pussy foot around, but to meet our problems head on and start solving them. How true! how true! Many put off problems, with the hope that they will disappear. That rarely happens. Instead, such problems tend to get bigger and bigger. What was once merely difficult to solve becomes a major issue requiring all of our attention and a great deal of resources. The other part of Halsey's advice is not to tenderly work your problem, but to take whatever steps are required boldly. Problems put off only become worse. Problems appeased with incomplete or tentative solutions remain problems.

Now your solutions may not work. That's normal, suggests Admiral Rickover. In complex situations, it would be very surprising if the first solution you tried worked every time. No big deal. Think of another solution.

If you are a leader, take care not to solve all of your subordinates' problems for them. Remember the reasons for delegation. They are true for problem solving, too. You'll soon be unable to keep up with all the problems brought to your attention. Sure, as General Smith suggests, you should help and provide guidance to your troops when appropriate. However, you should let them work out the solutions to their problems by themselves.

General "SLAM" Marshall reminds us that careful, analytical problem solving is fine, but not to throw out the good old fashion hunch either. There is strong scientific evidence to back up his suggestion. Researchers have discovered that the "gut feeling" sometimes used by executives is frequently right on target. Lucky guess? Not quite. The thinking is that executive's factor in a lifetime of experiences and that's where such hunches come from. So be sure to use all the analytical and computer-assisted problem-solving techniques at your disposal. However, if you have a strong hunch about something, you will often be right by going with your instincts, and not infrequently your instincts will be correct more often than the decisions based on quantitative analysis.

The wisdom of the generals about problem solving is:

* Confront your problems, never side-step them.

* If your first solution doesn't work, don't give up—try another.

* Train your subordinates to solve their own problems—give guidance only.

* Don't be afraid to follow your hunch.

PROMOTION

*I have heard of men peculiarly endowed by nature to be a general,
but I have never met one.*

GENERAL WILLIAM T. SHERMAN, U.S. Army

*We make generals today on the basis of their ability to write a
damned letter. Those kind of men can't get us ready for war.*

LIEUTENANT GENERAL LEWIS B. "CHESTY" PULLER, U.S. Marine Corps

*The men that can do things are going to be sought out just as
surely as the sun rises in the morning. Fake reputations, habits of glib
and clever speech, and glittering surface performance are going to be
discovered and kicked overboard.*

GENERAL OF THE ARMY DWIGHT D. EISENHOWER, U.S. Army

*As to rewards and promotion, it is essential to respect long service
and at the same time open a way for merit. . . . In time of war, however,
the regular order of promotion should be suspended, or at least reduced
to a third of the promotions, leaving the majority for brilliant conduct
and marked services.*

GENERAL HENRI DE JOMINI, French Army, Russian Army

*I kept command appointments in my own hand, right down to and
including battalion or regimental level. Merit, leadership and ability
were the sole criteria.*

FIELD MARSHAL BERNARD L. MONTGOMERY, British Army

We are all concerned about promotion, both our own and others.
General Sherman implies that there are no guarantees for any
to make the top. Moreover, those that are going to become senior executives are going to come from a variety of backgrounds, with a variety
of styles, beliefs, practices, and appearance.

General Puller cautions us about promoting people for the wrong
reasons. If we are going to make war, we want individuals as our

leaders who are particularly good at that function. If we have something else in mind, than those that have demonstrated their ability to do this other function are those we should promote.

Those who have made their reputations through fakery are going to be found out sooner or later . . . and the sooner the better. If we have the right personnel policies in operation it will be sooner. If not, then those who can't cut it will also be discovered, but its going to take longer and be at greater cost to the organization.

Accordingly, the policies that lead to promotion should be kept under constant review. When people are needed immediately for some important purpose, it's foolish to stick with those policies that worked well for us in the past, but in a vastly different environment and under very different conditions. Most organizations realize this. That is why wars sometimes see colonels and generals in their twenties and thirties when ages in the fifties, sixties, or even seventies were once the norm. This is also why we see so many young executives promoted by their companies in the age of e-commerce. Companies need managers that know their stuff and can compete effectively now, so the 25 year-old who can get the job done becomes a vice president and is promoted over a fine manager, with considerable seniority but doesn't have what is needed for a particular role. Critical situations required suspension of some of our standard promotion criteria.

If you want your organization to come out on top, you'd better follow Field Marshal Montgomery's advice and promote solely on the criteria of merit, leadership, and ability. Avoid any type of promotion on favoritism like the plague. With favoritism, not only will you get inferior people, but you will demoralize and probably lose the very good people you do not promote.

The wisdom from the generals on promotion is:

* No one is peculiarly endowed to reach the top—good leaders come from all sorts of backgrounds and look differently.
* Don't promote for the wrong reasons.
* Those who fake it will be found out—good personnel policies will bring this about quickly.
* Under emergency conditions, you need to amend your policies.
* Promote solely on merit, leadership, and ability—never favoritism.

RESPECT

He who feels the respect which is due to others cannot fail to inspire in them regard for himself, while he who feels, and hence manifests, disrespect towards others, especially his inferiors, cannot fail to inspire hatred against himself.

MAJOR GENERAL JOHN M. SCHOLFIELD, U.S. Army

World War II had taught me one important lesson in leadership: the most valuable soldier was one who was well-informed, encouraged to use his head, and treated with respect.

GENERAL OMAR N. BRADLEY, U.S. Army

Every great soldier has succeeded in convincing his men that he knows and respects them as individuals. To accomplish this end he goes among his men freely, mingling with them and giving the soldiers a chance to look him over and size him up. An officer who barricades himself behind his rank is properly suspected of having weaknesses to conceal—probably more than he actually has.

GENERAL MAXWELL D. TAYLOR, U.S. Army

The fundamental cause of any breakdown of morale and discipline within the Armed Forces usually comes of this—that a commander or his subordinates transgress by treating them as if they were children or serfs instead of showing respect for their adulthood.

BRIGADIER GENERAL S.L.A. MARSHALL, U.S. Army

There is a soul to an army as well as to the individual man, and no general can accomplish the full work of his army unless he commands the soul of his men as well as their bodies and legs.

GENERAL WILLIAM T. SHERMAN, U.S. Army

You cannot expect others to give you full support if you do not give them the respect that is due them. Yet some inexperienced leaders somehow think they are supposed to show disdain toward their subordinates. Some even think that showing disrespect towards their associates and minimum respect for their superiors somehow elevates them in the sight of others. Nothing could be further from the truth. Those you work with: subordinates, colleagues and superiors are all deserving of your respect. Treating them with anything less will reap the contempt and hatred that General Scholfield warns us against.

General Marshal goes so far as to state that not treating others with respect is the fundamental cause of any breakdown of morale and discipline in the organization. There is more to those who work for you then simply people earning a living.

When you are in charge, and you must motivate and influence them to do the best for the good of all, you must impact on that innermost stuff General Sherman refers to as their souls as well as their physical bodies or even their minds.

The wisdom of the generals regarding respect is:

* All deserve respect: those who work for you, those you work with, and those you work for.

* Fail to give respect and you will create hatred and contempt against yourself.

* Give respect to influence others to peak performance, and you will be able to reach their innermost being.

RESPONSIBILITY

Each commander must always assume total responsibility for every individual in his command. If the battalion or regimental commanders fail him in the attack, then he must relieve them or be relieved himself.

GENERAL OF THE ARMY OMAR N. BRADLEY, U.S. Army

When you do a deed, you bear responsibility for it.

MARSHAL OF THE SOVIET UNION GEORGI K. ZHUKOV, Soviet Army

It is a paramount and over-riding responsibility of every officer to take care of his men before caring for himself.

BRIGADIER GENERAL S.L.A. MARSHALL, U.S. Army

I tell you, as officers, that you will not eat, sleep, smoke, sit down, or lie down until your soldiers have had a chance to do these things. If you do this, they will follow you to the ends of the earth. If you do not, I will break you in front of your regiments.

FIELD MARSHAL SIR WILLIAM SLIM, British Army

A General Officer who will invariably assume the responsibility for failure, whether he deserves it or not, and invariably give credit for success to others, whether they deserve it or not, will achieve outstanding success.

GENERAL GEORGE S. PATTON, JR., U.S. Army

There is no getting around it. You are responsible for the actions of your organization, and those in it. But your responsibility always goes further. You most always take care of your people before you take care of yourself.

Field Marshal Slim elaborates on this. He says you shouldn't eat, sleep, smoke, sit down, or lie down until those reporting to you have a chance to do so. He says if you do this, they will follow you to the ends of the earth. He even threatens to fire those who fail to do this. I am well aware that you can give me numerous examples of leaders, some of them pretty good ones, who do not always follow this injunction. This is unfortunate. We all do what we have seen others do, and these leaders have seen no better as they moved up and were promoted. No one such as Field Marshal Slim made them aware of the full extent of their responsibilities. How much better leaders and how much more productive our organizations would have been had there been leaders to show them the way by example or explain to them what they must do. You can break the chain. You can set the example for others following you while building an organization with people that will follow you to the ends of the earth.

There is one more thing you must do to fulfill your full responsibility as a leader, and General Patton tells us what it is. When things go wrong and you are the leader, you must assume full responsibility, whether you deserve it or not. And when things go right, you must give full credit to others, again whether they fully deserve it or not. Do this, and you will achieve success as a leader.

- ★ A leader is responsible for everything his organization or members in it achieve or fail to achieve.
- ★ Your full responsibility means that you must always attend to the needs of those who report to you before your own.
- ★ When you encounter failure in your organization, take full responsibility; when you encounter success, give full credit to others.

RISK

Every attempt to make war easy and safe will result in humiliation and disaster.
GENERAL WILLIAM T. SHERMAN, U.S. Army

He who will not risk cannot win.
REAR ADMIRAL JOHN PAUL JONES, Continental Navy, Russian Navy

We had taken a calculated risk . . . I would rather be bold than wary even though wariness may sometimes be right.
GENERAL OF THE ARMY OMAR N. BRADLEY, U.S. Army

First reckon, then risk.
FIELD MARSHAL COUNT HELMUTH VON MOLTKE, German Army

Take calculated risks. That is quite different from being rash.
GENERAL GEORGE S. PATTON, JR., U.S. Army

No worthwhile activity is without risk. Life itself is not without risk. Without some risk, we cannot be successful. It is also true that sometimes the payoff is in direct proportion to the risk we accept.

The solution is not to try and make things risk-free. In almost all cases, that just can't be done at an acceptable cost. In some cases we get more trouble from trying to reduce risk to zero than simply accepting the risk and moving on. For example, it is possible to reduce the risk of an aircraft landing in bad weather by advanced types of precision radar both on the ground and on board the aircraft. However, the costs of these systems and the increased weight to the aircraft would at least double or triple the cost of commercial flying for the minimum number of accidents they would prevent.

If you read about the $10 light bulb and $600 toilet seat that the Department of Defense was buying some years ago, and you were wondering how the government could be so stupid, let me explain how.

A regular light bulb or toilet seat fails somewhere at a critical time and for whatever reason someone gets hurt or an aircraft is damaged. A commander or a congressman demands that we'll have no more of that. No good explaining that this was a million-to-one chance; unlikely to be repeated. Someone in power wants to assure his or her constituents and the media that he or she has fixed things so it will never happen again. Now, to ensure this light bulb won't fail under any conditions, it needs to be a special light bulb. Nobody makes them like that because there is no need. Also, testing to insure that this "armored" light bulb meets the new criteria adds more to the bill. When everything is done, you end up with "a gold-plated" light bulb, but yes, you have reduced the risk of failure to near zero. All is well and good until someone realizes the cost some years later and than we go back to the original 49 cent item again.

We can reduce or eliminate some risks, however, and we should. But, beyond a certain point we simply have to calculate the risks we take in any action. If they seem reasonable to us, we should accept them and press on.

Successful decisions tend to be bold decisions, as we discussed under that topic heading. However this does not mean that wariness does not have its place, too. And calculating and accepting the risk is much different from simply jumping in to any action without thinking at all. That type of rash behavior leads to disaster and failure more often than it leads to success.

Regarding risk, the wisdom of the generals is:

* ✶ All life involves risk, and you cannot become successful without risk.
* ✶ Calculate all risks before you take action—reduce or eliminate risks if you can, but if you can't and the risks are reasonable, press on!
* ✶ Successful decisions tend to be bold but this doesn't eliminate the requirement to be wary.
* ✶ Disregarding risk without consideration leads to disaster and failure.

POLICIES, RULES
AND REGULATIONS

Make no needless rules.

GENERAL ROBERT E. LEE, Confederate States Army

Any fool can keep a rule. God gave him a brain to know when to break the rule.

LIEUTENANT GENERAL WILLARD W. SCOTT, JR., U.S. Army

Regulations are very well for drill but in the hour of danger they are no more use . . . You must learn to think.

MARSHAL OF FRANCE FERDINAND FOCH, French Army

Method, I explained, was laid down in the Training Manuals, which were written not for sages, but for normal men, many of whom are fools. Though they must be followed, 'do not imagine for a moment,' I said, 'that they have been written to exonerate you from thinking.'

MAJOR GENERAL J.F.C. FULLER, British Army

What would my superiors direct, did they know what was passing under my nose?

ADMIRAL LORD NELSON, Royal Navy

No question about it, rules and policies are important. They save us a lot of time and trouble in having to consider each situation individually. But we have a brain to allow us to think and use our judgment. There are times when we must throw rules and policies out the window.

When the Japanese attacked Pearl Harbor on December 7th, 1941, we had a number of normal peacetime policies in place designed to protect lives and save equipment from waste and abuse. Ammunition and machine guns were kept under lock and key. A corporal was in charge, and the rule was that only the officer-of-the day had the authority to allow him to unlock the armory and issue the munitions. Picture this: the Japanese are attacking and dropping bombs. American soldiers and sailors are dying. Several soldiers head for the armory to get the guns and ammunition to fight back. But the corporal has his orders. He refuses to unlock the armory even though he knows an enemy is attacking. Think that didn't actually happen? It did.

I have seen at least as bad in civilian life, fortunately not with life and death consequences, although that too is possible. A business's computer system fails. The distributor is temporarily out of the needed part. It will take a week to get it. Meanwhile, the business will lose all sorts of money. The distributor has a used part which would work, but the policy manual says that used parts will not be used other than by the distributor. So the responsible manager tells the customer, "Sorry but . . ." I have seen airline clerks put passengers on a waiting list for a plane leaving hours later because policy would not permit a simple ticket change to a destination less than twenty miles from the original one.

All this is why we have to be very careful about the rules and policies we establish. Under certain conditions, we're going to have to scrap them, anyway, so we certainly don't want any needless ones.

Regarding the enforcement of rules and regulations, we need to remember that when they were developed no one imagined the present situation or, in Admiral Nelson's words, "what was passing under our noses."

As a young Air Force officer, I once sat on the source selection board to decide on the Advanced Warning and Control System (AWACS) multi-jet aircraft. One of the competitors asked to be relieved from a rule that an escape hatch had to be precisely so many inches by so many inches. If they could have changed this rule by a mere inch and a half, they could have saved us a million dollars on each aircraft. Of course, they would have been happy to qualify this modified hatch with a live drop to insure they weren't in any way compromising safety.

This sounded like a good deal to me, but one of the civilian members on the government team who had been around for a long time said that these rules were established for good reasons, and we shouldn't grant any modifications to them no matter what. However, he couldn't tell me where this particular rule came from. Since we had the time, I suggested we delay the decision a couple weeks to find out where this rule came from. The year was 1969, and we were talking about a jet aircraft traveling 400–500 miles per hour. This is significant, because believe it or not, we found that the rule came from some tests run in 1943 using the C-47, a propeller-driven aircraft with a top speed of maybe 150 miles per hour.

The wisdom of the generals on rules and policies:

  ✴ Rules are necessary—they can save us time, trouble, and resources.

  ✴ Don't make unnecessary rules, policies, or requirements.

  ✴ Never let the rule or policy interfere with using your head.

SELF-CONFIDENCE

The rules of conduct, the maxims of action, and the tactical instincts that serve to gain small victories may always be expanded into the winning of great ones with suitable opportunity.

ADMIRAL JOHN PAUL JONES, Continental Navy, Russian Navy

Fighting with a large army under your command is nowise different from fighting with a small one; it is merely a question of instituting signs and signals.

SUN TZU, Ancient Chinese General

Never take counsel of your fears.

LIEUTENANT GENERAL THOMAS JACKSON, Confederate States Army

When I think of the greatness of my job and realize that I am what I am, I am amazed, but on reflection, who is as good as I am? I know of no one.

GENERAL GEORGE S. PATTON, JR., U.S. Army

However desperate the situation, a senior commander must always exude confidence in the presence of his subordinates. For anxiety topside, can spread like cancer down through the command.

GENERAL OF THE ARMY OMAR BRADLEY, U.S. Army

Many individuals of high potential tell me they lack self-confidence. They want to know what they should do. In my experience, self-confidence grows from past success. The difficulty is many people's lack of self-confidence doesn't allow them much success. They think they are going to fail, so they do.

The solution is to start with small tasks that you know you can accomplish successfully. As you complete each successfully and develop more self-confidence, select more and more difficult tasks. In fact, as both John Paul Jones and Sun Tzu tell us, there really isn't a lot of difference between achieving a small victory and a large one. Well, as Sun Tzu says, maybe the signals are a little different.

A lot is based on our own fears. That's why General Jackson says not to listen to them. I am amazed at what individuals sometimes tell themselves which completely destroys their self-confidence. Here are some examples: "You've never done this before so you can't do it." "You're not smart enough." "You don't have the experience." "You are too young." "You are too old." It's really incredible. We are a lot harder on ourselves than anyone else would be.

If we want to build our self-confidence never say, "It's nothing" or anything like that when someone compliments us, even if we think it didn't take much effort. Just say, "Thank you." I know a man that no matter what he accomplishes, no matter how difficult, thinks if he can do it anyone can. And he says it was "easy," or "nothing." Big mistake. First, others may know it's not easy. So they think you are either some kind of nut, or are trying to put them down. More importantly for our self-confidence, we do nothing for it when we claim our victories required no effort. Maybe or maybe not, but we actually did them!

When he was Secretary of State, Henry Kissinger once disembarked from a plane after he had just concluded a difficult negotiation with the Soviets. An admirer rushed over to him and grasped his hand and gushed, "Dr. Kissinger, thank you for saving the world." Kissinger looked his admirer right in the eye and said, "Thank you." Now that's a demonstration of someone who has a lot of self-confidence. We have to smile a little about General Patton's self-confidence as well in being unable to think of anyone as great as he.

Am I recommending that we all become so egotistical? Not exactly. But many of us are capable of and may even have done great things. Yet, instead of telling ourselves that we are good, we tell ourselves the opposite.

The wisdom of the generals regarding self-confidence is:

* You can develop your self-confidence by starting with small victories.
* Understand that the difference in winning big victories and small ones is not very much.
* What you say or think is important—build yourself up, never tear yourself down.

SELF-CONTROL

A commander, besides commanding his armies, has got to learn how to command himself—which is not always too easy.

FIELD MARSHAL BERNARD L. MONTGOMERY, British Army

Only those who have discipline themselves can exact disciplined performance from others.

GENERAL MATTHEW B. RIDGWAY, U.S. Army

General Meade was an officer of great merit with drawbacks to his usefulness which were beyond his control . . . He made it unpleasant at times, even in battle, for those around him to approach him with information.

GENERAL ULYSSES S. GRANT, U.S. Army

I cannot trust a man to control others who cannot control himself.

GENERAL ROBERT E. LEE, Confederate States Army

To the man who is in terror and bordering on panic, no influence can be more steadying than that of seeing some other man near him who is retaining self-control and doing his duty.

BRIGADIER GENERAL S.L.A. MARSHALL, U.S. Army

In my observation of successful leaders and those that are less successful, self-control is high on my list of differences. Lack of self-control manifests itself in many ways. With some it is temper, with others, nervousness, some are prone to rumor-mongering, others making excuses . . . you name it. The tragedy is that frequently except for their lack of self-control, these are very capable individuals.

Field Marshal Montgomery says this isn't easy, but it is a must. "How can an undisciplined officer expect discipline from others," asks General Ridgway. General Grant is generous regarding General Meade. A capable officer, Grant calls him . . . but unfortunately one whom others would rather not be around, even with important information. Might Meade have succeeded at those battles in which he failed had he but exercised a little self-control? We can only speculate. General Lee, General Grant's main opponent during the Civil War gives us a much harsher judgment. He cannot even trust an officer to control others if he cannot control himself.

The interesting aspect of self-control, as General Marshall points out, is that it is contagious. This means that not only the leader, but anyone who demonstrates it can have an immediate and positive effect on stabilizing any situation that might otherwise result in panic and defeat.

The wisdom of the generals is:

* ★ Self-control is of great importance.
* ★ Self-control is not easy.
* ★ If you cannot control yourself, you cannot expect to control others.
* ★ Demonstrating self-control in the face of adversity can save the situation.

STRATEGY

I always make it a rule to get there first with the most men
LIEUTENANT GENERAL NATHAN BEDFORD FORREST, Confederate States Army

It is no use to get there first unless, when the enemy arrives, you also have the greater men—the greater force.
REAR ADMIRAL ALFRED THAYER MAHAN, U.S. Navy

My strategy is one against ten, my tactics ten against one.
FIELD MARSHAL ARTHUR WELLESLEY, The Duke of Wellington, English Army

The essence of strategy is, with a weaker army, always to have more force at the crucial point than the enemy.
NAPOLEON BONAPARTE, French Emperor

One of the guiding principles of fighting with an air force is assembling of weight by numbers, of a numerical concentration at decisive spots.
LIEUTENANT GENERAL ADOLF GALLANT, German Air Force

The basis of all strategy is to concentrate superior resources at the decisive point. General Forrest's words are sometimes quoted as "getting there firstest with the mostest." In either case, the thrust of General Forrest's comment is that you want to get there with your superior resources before your adversary can.

Two former advertising executives, Al Ries and Jack Trout have written a number of books that provide valuable insights into marketing. In one of these, *The 22 Immutable Laws of Marketing* (HarperBusiness 1993), they point out that companies or organizations that stake out their positions first are hard to displace. As proof, they take note of Hertz in car rental, IBM in main frame computers, and Coca Cola in soft drinks.

This is as good a place as any to point out the difference between strategy and tactics. Tactics are elements of strategy at the lowest level of operations. Thus your strategy may be where you are going to attack; your tactics how you are going to attack at that place. That's what Lord Wellington is talking about when he says his strategy is one against ten. His enemies may control ten different areas. He's not going to attack them all. He's going to concentrate his resources so that at the tactical level he has his adversary outnumbered ten to one.

The military has generally divided all strategy into three categories which have gone by different names over the years. For our purposes, I'll use the old names of grand strategy at the highest level, then strategy, then tactics. In business, some call the highest level strategic management, then strategy, and then tactics.

For example, let's say you make automobiles. You decide that at the strategic management level you decide there is an opportunity at the high end of the business, so you're going to put a lot of resources into expensive cars aimed at folks who have the money to buy them. At the next level down, marketing strategy, you decide to position your products as the most expensive in the market, and you want to be first into the market with some very innovative vehicles. Now your tactics need to support your strategy. You must build a very high quality product with lots of bells and whistles. You price it very high. You don't want to price it low even if you can make money at a low price. Why? Because it won't have "the most expensive in the market" image you are looking for. For distribution, pick only the wealthier parts of town with distributors that are willing to put a lot of money into very fancy showrooms. Finally, if you want to do a direct mail campaign, don't use inexpensive black and white brochures, go first-class with full color, high quality, glossy paper. And your mailing list . . . make sure it includes only those making enough money to afford your car. Don't waste money sending it to others.

Now let's get back into how to concentrate our resources. We don't have an unlimited budget. No one has. That's why we don't send brochures to every name we can find. It is also why we decided to sell only to this relatively small very wealthy market. You can't concentrate everywhere and be everything to everybody. That's what the generals figured out, and that's what successful business people must do. In fact, this basic concept of strategy works in everything including romance.

Some years ago in some research I did in strategy, I found a man who "won" his spouse over a competitor by finding a way to concentrate and spend more time with her than his rival did.

About strategy, the wisdom of the generals is:

* ✷ Concentrate superior resources at the decisive point.

* ✷ Get to the decisive point before your competitor.

* ✷ Make certain that your tactics fit and support your strategy and that your strategy fits and supports your grand strategy.

STRESS

Living with stress, knowing how to handle pressure, is necessary for survival. It is related to a man's ability to wrest control of his own destiny from the circumstances that surround him.

VICE ADMIRAL JAMES B. STOCKDALE, U.S. Navy

The military . . . puts stresses upon men such as they have not known elsewhere, and the temptation to "get out from under" would be irresistible if their spirits had not been tempered to the ordeal.

BRIGADIER GENERAL S.L.A. MARSHALL, U.S. Army

Experience had also taught me that if you lay your plans in detail before you are under the stress of fighting, the chances are much greater that you will be able to implement at least the outlines of the plans despite the contingencies of battle.

MAJOR GENERAL ARIEL SHARON, Army of Israel

The general is dealing with men's lives, and must have a certain mental robustness to stand the strain of this responsibility.

FIELD MARSHAL ARCHIBALD P. WAVELL, British Army

Avoiding needless pressure on a individual is almost always in the best interest of the unit.

MAJOR GENERAL AUBREY NEWMAN, U.S. Army

Stress goes hand in hand with modern living and working as well as warfare. Stress-related illnesses range across the board and have been correlated not only to the onset of heart disease, headaches, and mental problems, but also to the less obvious and most serious ones, including cancer.

Of course, not all stress is bad. In fact, scientists have discovered that too little stress in our lives may be as bad as too much, since too little stress can lead to boredom and, like too much stress, to depression.

There are two basic approaches for dealing with stress, whatever its source. The first is to reduce or avoid it. We can accomplish this by exercising more control over our lives. General Sharon's injunction regarding planning before becoming engaged is a prime example. Planning in all phases of our life also helps us by avoiding trying to accomplish too much with insufficient time and in learning which activities to accept and which to avoid.

The other is to learn how to handle stress. When the generals speak of mental robustness and tempering, they are talking about our innate ability to deal with the stress in our lives that we cannot reduce or avoid. Vacations, short breaks in our schedule, hot baths, meditation, and mental and feedback training are all methods of developing ourselves to better withstand the effects of stress with which we are confronted.

General Newman cautions us that when we ourselves are in control of a situation, we should not put unnecessary pressure on those who report to us. This advice is not only one for the health of our people, but also to maximize productivity. Here again, we can go overboard. Both too little pressure and too much can limit productivity. Too much pressure can cause the individual to close down mentally and simply give up. Too little causes boredom and lethargy and a tendency to do too little. Neither extreme is healthy when it comes to stress.

The wisdom of the generals regarding stress:

* Too much stress can cause a variety of undesired consequences to both health and productivity.

* We can learn to avoid or reduce unwanted stress.

* We can learn to deal with stress that cannot be avoided or reduced.

* As a manager, we must not put unnecessary pressure on those who work for us—too much and too little are both bad.

SUCCESS

There are no secrets to success; don't waste time looking for them . . . You must be ready for opportunity when it comes.

GENERAL COLIN POWELL, U.S. Army

Although I cannot insure success, I will endeavor to deserve it.

ADMIRAL JOHN PAUL JONES, Continental Navy, Russian Navy

To move swiftly, strike vigorously, and secure all the fruits of the victory is the secret of successful war.

MAJOR GENERAL THOMAS JACKSON, Confederate States Army

In war, many roads lead to success, and they do not all involve the opponent's defeat.

MAJOR GENERAL KARL VON CLAUSEWITZ, Prussian Army

Success is disarming . . . there is apt to ensure laxness in all its forms and with all its dangers.

BRIGADIER GENERAL S.L.A. MARSHALL, U.S. Army

One definition of success is attainment of a worthwhile goal. Admiral Jones and General Powell both tell us that success cannot be guaranteed. However, they both give us ways that increase our chances of attaining it. General Powell says that we must be ready for the opportunity. This implies preparation. How can we prepare? We can prepare by obtaining the right education and training. We can prepare by planning so that we understand what we must do. We can prepare by seeking positions that lead where we want to go according to our definition of "a worthwhile goal."

Admiral Jones' approach is the other half of General Powell's preparation. He says that we must take the actions that deserve success. How can we do this? We can work hard at whatever task is assigned us no matter how undesirable the work may be. We can seek and volunteer for additional work above the minimum required. We can learn the jobs of others so that we understand how our work fits in with theirs and can substitute for them if needed.

General Jackson elaborates on how to perform actions which are deserving of success. He suggests that we move swiftly, strike vigorously, and secure all the fruits of the victory, the latter meaning the exploitation of success we discussed in an earlier section. This means that in taking these actions, we must not hesitate or delay, but as multi-billionaire W. Clements Stone says, "Do it now!"

General Clausewitz points out that no single path leads to success, nor does veering off in any particular direction necessarily lead to failure. If becoming a general is your definition of success, than consider this. Lieutenant General Longstreet, General Lee's "warhorse" during the Civil War was a paymaster before the war. Panzer Leader Heinz Guderian ran a communications vehicle as a junior officer early in his career. Army General Frederick Kroesen who retired as Commanding General, U.S. Army Europe was once in charge of Army Recruiting. While his classmates were in combat assignments in France during World War I, Eisenhower was stuck in training in the States. There is an infinite number of roads to success, and as General Clausewitz says, they may not even involve an opponent's defeat.

In our last quotation, General Marshall cautions us about success; that it can lead to laxness, with all its dangers. Living in the Los Angeles area and not too far from Hollywood, I am constantly being made aware of once very successful movie or television stars who fell victim to this very danger and lost everything. Some are in jail, some have serious drug problems, and many have lost their fortunes and are now paupers. Don't let this happen to you! When you have reached that worthwhile goal and you wear the mantle of success, don't rest on your laurels. Pick a new worthwhile goal and achieve even more success.

The wisdom of the generals regarding success is:

★ If you want success, prepare yourself for it.

★ If you want success, make yourself deserving of it.

★ Don't be concerned about a particular path or incident ruining your chances of achieving success—there are many pathways, some are convoluted.

★ Once you achieve success, pick a new worthwhile goal and keep moving on.

SURPRISE

The technique for military conquest is to carefully investigate the enemy's intentions and quickly take advantage of them, launching a sudden attack where unexpected.

(T'AI KUNG) CHIANG SHANG, Ancient Chinese General

The two factors that produce surprise are secrecy and speed.

MAJOR GENERAL CARL VON CLAUSEWITZ, Prussian Army

Rapidity is the essence of war; take advantage of the enemy's unreadiness, make your way by expected routes, and attack unguarded spots.

SUN TZU, Ancient Chinese General

Whatever a thing may be, be it pleasant or terrible, the less it has been foreseen the more it pleases or frightens. This is seen nowhere better than in war, where surprise strikes terror even in those who are much the stronger party.

XENOPHON, Ancient Greek General

You will usually find that the enemy has three courses open to him, and of these he will adapt the fourth.

FIELD MARSHAL HELMUTH VON MOLKE, German Army

Surprise is an important element of competitive strategy which you must master and use to your advantage against competitors if you are to be successful. As T'ai Kung Chiang Shang notes, it simply requires us to do the unexpected. Yet accomplishment of that simple task may require considerable subterfuge and sophistication. Speed and secrecy are primary. In that way we can take advantage of our competitors' lack of preparation and readiness for our actions. We can also create surprise in the manner in which we do things, or at the place or timing of them as we do them. We can also create a diversion to give the impression we are going to do something or at someplace we are not.

Prior to the landings at the planned beachheads in Normandy during World War II, the allies launched all sorts of deceptions to mislead and surprise the enemy as to the time and place of the attack, which the Germans knew must come.

In one deception, an entire fake army group supposedly under the command of Patton was set up in England. With fake encampments and equipment that could be photographed from the air, and electronic communications which could be monitored by the Germans, the "army group" was in place and acting normally in England even as the allied landings were under way.

Another hoax for D-Day in Normandy was the creation of a fake major, whose body was allowed to wash ashore on neutral, but fascist-leaning Spain, with important documents pertaining to D-Day which marked false beaches for the landings.

Through these actions, the Germans misallocated their forces and Hitler delayed in taking action against the real landings, thinking these were the false ones. They were surprised. By using such techniques, even if competitors know what we are going to do, we can still create surprise.

Of course, surprise applies to all competitive situations, not just warfare. In an interview during my research on strategy, an executive shared this story with me. In college, he had been a champion swimmer. However, a competitor on the opposing team was faster overall. His own advantage had always been that he had the capability of an exceptionally strong finish. The strategy he decided on was not far off from that demonstrated by the story of the tortoise and the hare. He decided not to go out and push his opponent, but to allow him an easy lead in the first part of the race. In that way, he would lull his opponent into complacency. With only yards remaining, he used his stronger finish to pull ahead and win over his opponent who normally had a much faster time over the overall course.

It goes without saying that we don't want to be surprised by anything our competitor may do. Moreover, Xenophon tells us that the more we can foresee, the less apprehensive we will be. Von Molke's admonition is merely a cautionary note: that preparing for an adversary's alternatives is not necessarily the easiest thing in the world.

The wisdom of the generals on surprise is:

★ Surprise is an important and necessary element of strategy.

★ We gain surprise through doing the unexpected.

★ We gain the unexpected through speed and secrecy, and deception as to manner, place, or timing.

★ We must expend equal effort to avoid being surprised ourselves.

TACT

Always be tactful and well-mannered and teach your subordinates to be the same. Avoid excessive sharpness or harshness of voice, which usually indicates the man who has shortcomings of his own to hide.

FIELD MARSHAL ERWIN ROMMEL, German Army

There is no substitute for empathy—for understanding the viewpoints and situations of others—when deciding how direct you can be in your dealings with others.

MAJOR GENERAL AUBREY NEWMAN, U.S. Army

Man, not men, is the most important consideration.

NAPOLEON BONAPARTE, Emperor of France

If the approach to the human factor is cold and impersonal, than you achieve nothing.

FIELD MARSHAL BERNARD MONTGOMERY, British Army

I feel that retired general officers should never miss an opportunity to remain silent concerning matters for which they are no longer responsible.

GENERAL H. NORMAN SCHWARZKOPF, U.S. Army

The few senior officers I have known who lack tact are conspicuous because of their small number. When I was a young high school cadet in ROTC, an old sergeant told me that the higher in rank an officer, the more pleasant his personality. Throughout my career I found this to be true, and as I myself advanced in rank, I realized that there was an important reason for this. Senior ranking officers had more and more need for tact in dealing with people at all levels in their organizations and in other organizations as well. Without tact, this made it very difficult to get things done.

Now, I don't mean that you don't occasionally need to reprimand or correct subordinates. But there are many ways of doing this and still getting the job done. Steel Magnate Andrew Carnegie was the richest man in the country when he surprised two of his workers smoking right next to a large sign in one of his factories which read "No Smoking!" His way of reprimanding them was to take two cigars from his jacket. Handing them the cigars, he said. "Boys, would you mind smoking these in another area? We can have a fire here, and it sets a bad example for others."

Even the Emperor Napoleon said that he didn't blow up when thwarted. He held his tongue, and he tells us that it is the individual man, not men, who is important.

If our approach is cold and impersonal—tactless—than we achieve nothing. So says, Field Marshal Montgomery, victor at El Alamein. Marine General Louis Wilson who was Commandant of the U.S. Marine Corps in the 1970s always reminded his Marines to reprimand in private, never in public. That's tact!

We close with a quote from General Schwarzkopf, who lets us know that tact sometimes simply means keeping our mouths shut.

Here is the wisdom of the generals on tact:

* Be tactful to everyone.
* If you feel frustrated, don't let off steam on others, follow the Emperor Napoleon's advice, and hold your tongue.
* Criticize in private and praise in public.
* Sometimes tact is keeping your mouth shut.

TEAMWORK

Troops should not be encouraged to foster a spirit of jealousy and unjust detraction toward other arms of the service, where all are mutually dependent and mutually interested, with functions differing in character, but not in importance.

MAJOR GENERAL J.E.B. STUART, Confederate States Army

The teams and staffs through which the modern commander absorbs information and exercises his authority must be a beautifully interlocked, smooth-working mechanism. Ideally, the whole should be practically a single mind.

GENERAL OF THE ARMY DWIGHT D. EISENHOWER, U.S. Army

Our military forces are on one team—in the game to win regardless of who carries the ball.

GENERAL OF THE ARMY OMAR N. BRADLEY, U.S. Army

Successful fighter tactics against enemy threats depend upon intricate and cooperative teamwork—the basic reason for the team approach in the first place. They also depend on each member operating with that team concept at all times.

GENERAL WILBUR L. CREECH, U.S. Air Force

An Army is a team. It eats, sleeps, lives and fights as a team. All this stuff you've been hearing about individuality is a bunch of crap.

GENERAL GEORGE S. PATTON, JR., U.S. Army

Hollywood frequently likes to emphasize the individual lone wolf. It is Rambo, Superman, or James Bond who are the heroes. This is usually not true on the battlefield, not true in sports, and not true in business operations either. Teamwork is the proven key to success.

We can use friendly competition between different units in an organization to encourage productivity. However, we must be very careful not to develop a spirit of jealousy between different functions or units. That's totally destructive to teamwork.

Unfortunately this can happen because we are trying to raise the morale of a particular group. For example, when Steve Jobs, founder of Apple hired John Sculley to run the company, he took over responsibilities for the MacIntosh project. However, the Apple Computer was still the cash cow, earning most of the company's profits. Jobs, in seeking to raise the morale of his division would call those in the Apple division "members of the very boring project." Now, this would be okay for good-natured rivalry except that Jobs was a founder; too powerful a figure. It was demoralizing to those not in his MacIntosh Division and could not fail to have a negative impact on the rest of the organization.

The equivalent in the military would be if a service chief obviously favored one of the specialties in his organization over others. This has happened, and when it does, it invariably creates the jealousies Jackson speaks about and destroys teamwork.

Our goal should be to encourage teamwork whenever we can. We can take some lessons from the U.S. Marine Corps in this respect. Every Marine is required to go through the same basic infantry course regardless of the specialty in which they are to be employed. If you ask a Marine what he or she does, the answer will be, "I'm a Marine." This is not necessarily so in other services. You may get an answer, "I'm a fighter pilot," or "I'm an infantry officer," or "I'm a submariner." As I said, it is the Marines who have it right in this instance.

You want your organization, no matter how big, to be a team. You want it to think, act, and win as a team. Anything less, as General Patton says, is a bunch of crap.

The wisdom of the generals regarding teamwork is:

* All parts of your organization, regardless of function, department or specialty are on the same team.
* Avoid encouraging a spirit of jealousy.
* Do encourage teamwork in every way you can.
* Anything less than teamwork is counterproductive.

TIME

Time is the essence in war . . . days and hours—even minutes—frittered away can never be regained.

BRIGADIER GENERAL SAMUEL B. GRIFFITH II, U.S. Marine Corps

In military operations, time is everything.

FIELD MARSHAL ARTHUR WELLESLEY, The Duke of Wellington, British Army

Time is everything; five minutes makes the difference between victory and defeat.

ADMIRAL LORD HORATIO NELSON, Royal Navy

A good solution applied with vigor now is better than a perfect solution ten minutes later.

GENERAL GEORGE S. PATTON, JR., U.S. Army

A few hours later will be too late. Delay means disaster: resolute, energetic and immediate action means success.

MAJOR GENERAL F.W. MELLENTHIN, German Army

Time is a commodity that, once gone, cannot be recaptured. That is what General Griffith tells us, and it requires little reflection to see that it is true. Before his death, Bruce Catton, the famed Civil War historian and writer spoke to a group of upper class cadets at West Point. He urged his audience not to waste a single moment. He told them that even while shaving in the morning he went over notes in preparation for his writing or research of the day. He said that when young, we operate on the erroneous assumption of immortality and unlimited time. Now, nearing the close of life, he knew his future accomplishments had a time limit governing them and that time, immeasurably valuable, was also strictly limited.

Time is limited for any purpose. Sometimes it doesn't take much to mean the difference between success and failure. A friend of mine sold life insurance. There was a potentially big client that we both knew but my friend was actually afraid to approach him. The weeks slipped by as my friend tried to build up the courage to ask for an appointment. Finally he was able to do it. He made an appointment and visited our mutual friend only to discover that this individual would have been more than ready to purchase from him, but had already signed up for an extremely large policy the day before.

There are hundreds of stories like this. You are probably as familiar as I am with them. Why then, do we hesitate? Why do we not recognize the immense and critical value of time and act at once.

One reason is fear. Like my friend who needed time to build up his courage to act. The fear prevented him from reaching his goal.

Another reason is the assumption that we can always do it. An acquaintance of mine is an editor with a large textbook publishing house. He told me that the main reason that professors never go on contract to do a textbook, is not that they cannot write, but that they can. He explained, that because they write well they are busy publishing articles for academic journals, they assume a publishing company will always be ready to publish a textbook they might write. However, this isn't true. The investment in a new textbook is so enormous and the risk of failure so great that multiple editions for a successful book out into the future is required. Any publisher of college textbooks wants younger authors so they can be assured of a new edition incorporating the latest information for years to come. With older authors, they must stop to consider whether or not this will be possible.

A third reason why we let time slip away is because we are waiting for things to be perfect. We want all the information, we want more resources, we want the relationship to be just so. Unfortunately, perfection is an illusion. It never comes. Only resolute, energetic and immediate action brings success.

The wisdom of the generals about time is:

★ Time is an irreplaceable commodity—don't waste it.

★ Very small units of time . . . days, hours, even minutes . . . can be the difference between success and failure.

★ Resolute, energetic and immediate action leads to success.

TRAINING

In no other profession are the penalties for employing untrained personnel so appalling or so irrevocable as in the military.

GENERAL OF THE ARMY DOUGLAS MACARTHUR, U.S. Army

The fundamental purpose of all training today is to develop the natural faculties and stimulate the brain of the individual rather than to treat him as a cog that has to be fitted into a great machine.

BRIGADIER GENERAL S.L.A. MARSHALL, U.S. Army

My troops are good and well-disciplined, and the most important thing of all is that I have thoroughly habituated them to perform everything they are required to execute. You will do something more easily, to a higher standard, and more bravely when you know that you will do it well.

FREDERICK THE GREAT, German Emperor

It makes no difference how fine your weapons are, or how competent your leaders, if the men in the ranks are not physically hardened and highly skilled, you do not have an effective fighting force.

GENERAL MATTHEW B. RIDGWAY, U.S. Army

The best form of "welfare" for the troops is first class training, for this saves unnecessary casualties.

FIELD MARSHAL ERWIN ROMMEL, German Army

Training prepares us to face the real challenges in our professions, whatever our professions may be. Despite the fact that practically all agree that we are in the most demanding times ever, with strong competition of the highest order at the local, national, and international level, many organizations spend too little time in training, or don't train at all.

Yet the cost of a single mistake may be catastrophic to the organization. I once worked with a company that had screwed up three government research and development contracts in a row. Yet their screw-ups were not because the people didn't know their stuff technically, or weren't working hard, or trying hard, but simply because the company didn't send its key people for some basic training regarding contracting with the federal government. Their mistakes came close to causing the company to go under.

There are all sorts of reasons why training may be considered unnecessary. "It costs too much." "It takes too much time from our real activities." "We have too much turnover, so we'd just be conducting training for our competitors." "We train by doing." "We hired people that have the know-how."

All of these excuses are pretty lame. Good training will pay back every dollar invested. If lack of training is causing mistakes during "real activities," time training with no penalties for mistakes will save money overall. Maybe one reason the company has such a high rate of turnover is lack of success due to insufficient training. You can't train by doing without paying a heavy price. By then, it's too late. Knowledge is expanding, and technical development occurring at such a high rate, that no one who is not periodically trained is up-to-date.

In this day of Drucker's "knowledge worker," training is more important than ever. Poor training today doesn't mean just a machine on the production line goes down. It could mean your entire computer system crashes and you are essentially out of business in the interim. So regardless of your industry, planned technical, management, process, sales or whatever training on an on-going basis is essential.

The wisdom of the generals on training:

* A pint of training will save a gallon of mistakes and a ton of money.
* The fact that you've hired great people, built great facilities, and bought great equipment counts for naught if you don't keep those great people trained.
* The best form of insurance your company can invest in is first rate training.
* People will do better and perform at a higher standard when they know they can do it well—this comes from training.

TRUST

We earn and sustain the respect and trust of the public and of our troops because of the integrity and self-discipline we demonstrate. Officers should strive to develop forthright integrity—officers who do the right thing in their professional and private lives—and have the courage to take responsibility for their choices.

GENERAL RONALD R. FOGLEMAN, U.S. Air Force

Not only the future of our arms but the well-being of our people depend upon a constant reaffirmation and strengthening of public faith in the virtue and trustworthiness of the officer body.

BRIGADIER GENERAL S.L.A. MARSHALL, U.S. Army

An army fearful of its officers is never as good as one that trusts and confides in its leaders.

GENERAL OF THE ARMY DWIGHT D. EISENHOWER, U.S. Army

No matter what may be the ability of the officer, if he loses the confidence of his troops, disaster must sooner or later ensue.

GENERAL ROBERT E. LEE, Confederate States Army

There is an old saying: "Trust everybody, but cut the cards." In command, staff, and leadership this translates to: "Trust everybody, but check the facts in things that matter."

MAJOR GENERAL AUBREY NEWMAN, U.S. Army

Trust has to be earned and as we have seen earlier, trust is closely bound up with integrity. We earn trust by demonstrating our integrity as leaders . . . by doing the right thing. Trust is so important in building top performing organizations and getting others to follow our lead that it is no exaggeration, as General Marshall proclaims, that the entire future of our arms and our country depend on it. It is the most valuable coin any leader possesses.

Once you win this trust, you can do almost anything. Without trust it is very difficult to operate. When I first went to work in industry, I got a job as head of research and development for a company building pilot helmets and oxygen masks. When I took over, I called my project engineers together. One of the things I told them was that if they disagreed with me, I wanted them to tell me plainly. I might still decide to do what I intended, but then again, after listening to their arguments, I might not. However, if they said nothing, I would do what I intended anyway, and if things went awry because of this decision I would assume that they were just as dumb as I.

They laughed when I told them this, but few took me up on it for several weeks. They were afraid of what I might do. I had to build trust first. Once I did, they told me what they thought regardless of how much they believed I thought I was right. That's the way I wanted it. Right up until the time I made a decision, if they disagreed, I expected them to vigorously (but courteously) oppose my viewpoint. Once, I made a decision, or we made one together, I expected everyone to jump on board and implement it to the best of their ability. They did, and it brought us much success. The whole thing was based on trust. That coin was of such value that I couldn't have put a price on it.

And General Lee is quite correct. Once we lose this trust, we court disaster no matter what other abilities we might possess.

General Newman points out that while we want to give others the same trust, we don't want to be a Pollyanna either. This means that though we have full trust, we are still responsible and would be foolish not to spot check things that are very important.

The wisdom of the generals regarding trust is:

* Trust between you and those who work for you is a valuable coin—build it and spend it wisely.

* You build trust based on integrity—do the right thing, always!

* Once you lose the trust of others, you're going to have problems regardless of what other abilities you possess.

* Trust others as they trust you, but this doesn't relieve you of responsibility, so check on the things that count anyway.

VALUES

I have concluded that we were put on this earth for a purpose. That purpose is to make it, within our capabilities, a better place in which to live.
GENERAL JAMES "JIMMY" DOOLITTLE, U.S. Air Force

It should be perfectly clear that any institution must know what its ideals are before it can become coherent and confident . . .
BRIGADIER GENERAL S.L.A. MARSHALL, U.S. Army

Duty—Honor—Country. Those three hallowed words reverently dictate what you ought to be, what you can be, what you will be.
GENERAL OF THE ARMY DOUGLAS MACARTHUR, U.S. Army

It is the duty of commanding officers in every echelon to develop to the highest degree the conditions and influences calculated to promote the health, morals, and spiritual values of the personnel under their command.
GENERAL OF THE ARMY GEORGE C. MARSHALL, U.S. Army

We have become convinced of the need to continually articulate the core values of our institution. These ideals are at the heart and soul of our military profession: integrity first, service before self, and excellence in all we do.
GENERAL RONALD R. FOGLEMAN, U.S. Air Force

An organization without values is like a sailboat adrift on the ocean without a rudder. Depending on the wind, it goes first one way, and then another. Any organization worth its salt has values which drive it and which it carefully guards. As General Doolittle says, we were put on this earth to contribute and make it a better place to live. Our values help define our contributions and the manner in which they are made.

That was what was wrong with the antagonist, a brilliant and effective Marine Corps colonel played by Jack Nicholson in the movie,

A Few Good Men. Tom Cruise, playing a young Navy attorney, exposes the colonel whose lying and disobedience to orders has caused the death of one of his Marines. Angered, the colonel tells Cruise that since he is in the business of defending civilians and others like Tom Cruise who are not real warriors, Cruise has no right to challenge the manner in which he provides this defense. This argument rejects the very values of the military services and those of the United States Marine Corps. General Marshall says that every organization must know and understand its ideals (values) before it can become coherent and confident. You can bet the Marine Corps does. As General MacArthur says to the Corps of Cadets about the West Point values: "Duty—Honor—Country. Those three hallowed words reverently dictate what you ought to be, what you can be, what you will be."

It is the responsibility of managers at every level to articulate and promote the values of an organization. And it is well to document them. About 1995, when General Fogleman was Chief of Staff of the Air Force, the Air Force did not have its values documented. General Fogleman formed a committee of senior Air Force generals to uncover and make recommendations as to the basic values that should drive the U.S. Air Force in carrying out its mission. The committee came up with three values which were adopted and which are stated by General Fogleman in his quotation. It would be well for every organization to document what it is that it believes in.

The wisdom of the generals regarding values is:

* ⋆ The purpose of an organization is to contribute—how this is accomplished is of equal importance.
* ⋆ It is the responsibility of managers at every level to articulate and promote the organization's values.
* ⋆ If the values in your organization are not yet written down, it would be well to do so.

VICTORY

From the Far East I send you one single thought, one sole idea—written in red on every beachhead from Australia to Tokyo—there is no substitute for Victory!

GENERAL DOUGLAS MACARTHUR, U.S. Army

Whoever wants to keep alive must aim at victory. It is the winners who do the killing and the losers who get killed.

XENOPHON, Ancient Greek General

All my care will be to gain victory with the least shedding of blood.

NAPOLEON BONAPARTE, French Emperor

They're on our right, they're on our left, they're in front of us, they're behind us; they can't get away from us this time.

LIEUTENANT GENERAL LEWIS B. PULLER, U.S. Marine Corps

There is only one decisive victory: the last.

MAJOR GENERAL KARL VON CLAUSEWITZ, Prussian Army

Victory is the ultimate success, or at least the ultimate success in a category of successes in a struggle or endeavor against odds. What General MacArthur is telling us is that no matter how you look at things in life, there is no substitute for it. You can fight the good fight and lose honorably. Sometimes we must do this. But it in no way compares with achieving the high attainment of victory.

In war, Xenophon explains why: it is the winners who do the killing and the losers who get killed. In ancient times this was frequently an accurate description of what happened. The gist of what he is saying is true, even today. The victors benefit greatly, and those who are defeated suffer significant losses.

At the Olympics, after years of training and a lifetime of commitment, the top three winners get medals, the others nothing. But this is sport, and participation, in itself, is a benefit, as is the honor of competing. The differences between victory and defeat in other arenas are much greater. Victors gain more professional opportunities and additional work and chances to contribute. Victors gain in knowledge and opportunities. Victors gain wealth and celebrity, Victors gain the mates of their choice. Victors gain vacation homes and travel abroad. Victors gain the good things in life. All in all, victory is nothing to be sniffed at.

Nothing comes in life without payment, and it is Napoleon who cautions us to insure that the victory is bought at the minimum costs. To me this price must be wary of what is taken from our personal relationships, especially with our families. What good is it if we reach the top with a score of great victories to our credit, if it is bought with the coin of our spouses and children? I know of a very famous man, a hero of mine, but neither in the military nor in business. His many victories had brought him international fame and success, but at great cost: the neglect of his children. They suffered enormous problems in life brought about as a price for his victories.

General Puller points out that there are many definitions of victory, and at times a victory may in fact be what in other situations may be viewed as a defeat. Similarly, it is the final victory that counts, not the smaller defeats along the way. We suffered many defeats in our battle with our mother country, England, before finally gaining our independence after Washington won the Battle of Yorktown in 1781.

Colonel Harry Summers talked with his opposite number, Colonel Tu, during a break in negotiating with the North Vietnamese over the release of our captured prisoners in Hanoi in 1972. "Colonel Tu, you never once beat us on the battlefield," said Colonel Summers. Summers said that Tu considered this comment for a moment and than replied, "It may be so, but it is irrelevant."

The wisdom of the generals about victory is:

* There is no substitute for victory.
* There is a price to be paid for it, and we should ensure it is minimal.
* It is only the final victory that counts.

VISION

*Victory smiles upon those who anticipate the changes in the
character of war, not upon those who wait to adapt themselves after
they occur.*

MAJOR GENERAL GIULIO DOUHET, Italian Air Force

*Leaders must provide vision. Leaders who are not planners are
simply caretakers and gatekeepers.*

MAJOR GENERAL PERRY. M. SMITH, U.S. Air Force

*If I always appear prepared, it is because before entering an
undertaking, I have meditated for long and have foreseen what may
occur. It is not genius which reveals to me suddenly and secretly what I
should do in circumstances unexpected by others, It is thought and meditation.*

NAPOLEON BONAPARTE, French Emperor

*No one starts a war—or rather, no one in his senses ought to do
so—without first being clear in his mind what he intends to achieve by
that war and how he intends to conduct it.*

MAJOR GENERAL KARL VON CLAUSEWITZ, Prussian Army

*Any air force which does not keep its doctrine ahead of its equip-
ment, and its vision far into the future, can only delude the nation into a
false sense of security.*

GENERAL OF THE AIR FORCE HENRY H. ARNOLD, U.S. Air Force

Vision has to do with laying out the future in our imagination. We
anticipate the future of what is to come through our imaginations, and prepare for it. Those who do this are the real leaders. Others
who wait merely to adapt to the vision of others are followers: caretakers and gatekeepers even though they may bear responsibilities or title
as leaders.

Napoleon practiced his profession with such vision that he was
thought to have some special power or genius for predicting the future.

Here, he tells us his secret. It is simply thought and meditation, the necessary ingredients of vision.

General Clausewitz cautions us not to embark on any serious enterprise without first being clear in our minds regarding our vision for the outcome. General Arnold concurs that not keeping our visions updated and far into the future at best leads us into a false sense of security, the implications of this being extremely negative.

About vision, the wisdom of the generals is:

⋆ Anticipation through vision will save you from much of the expense of changes due to mistakes later.

⋆ Vision comes from thought and meditation, not genius.

⋆ Don't embark until you image it through in your minds first.

⋆ Keep your vision updated into the future.

PART III

THE AFTER ACTION REPORT:

THE CONTRIBUTORS
AND WHAT THEY DID

"I don't know who won the Battle of the Marne, but if it had been lost, I know who would have lost it."

—MARSHAL OF FRANCE JOSEPH JOFFRE

The contributors to *Wisdom of the Generals* come from every age and every country and all military services. The sole criterion used was that the contributors achieved flag rank (that is general or admiral), that they were primarily military men, and that the insight they rendered was important to the topic discussed.

No doubt, there were others who might be considered more important using historical criteria. But that was not the criterion used for selection. Moreover, I made no attempt at balance when it came to politics or controversy.

As a result, I excluded political leaders, unless they were formerly generals or admirals. Thus I included George Washington and Napoleon Bonaparte, but excluded Abraham Lincoln and Winston Churchill, although both Lincoln and Churchill had served as officers in battle, but neither became a general nor an admiral. Moreover, for generals-turned-politicians, I used their military, not their political titles. Thus I quoted Eisenhower as "General of the Army Eisenhower," not "President Eisenhower."

However, there were exceptions to this. Many historical figures, especially ancients, are so well known that their military titles make them sound bizarre. So I quoted Xenophon and Sun Tzu, rather than General Xenophon or General Sun Tzu. Also, some of these ancients and some modern generals never held the title of general, even though they performed this function. Mao Tse-tung comes to mind as one example. The Peoples Liberation Army didn't use military ranks in his day. Originally, Chinese communist "ranks" were only two: "fighter" or "commander." So I quoted Mao without the honorific.

I also excluded several influential military philosophers who gained their wisdom and wrote their conclusions not by practicing, but by observing warfare and synthesizing the experiences of others. Vegetius was probably the most outstanding example of this excluded category.

Sometimes strange things happen in trying to get the ranks right in English. For example, when Moshe Dayan was Chief of Staff of the Israeli Army, the equivalent of his rank "rav aluf" was major general. There was only one, and it was he. Some years after he retired, an additional rank was added. The new rank (tat aluf) is the equivalent of brigadier general. The former brigadier general equivalent rank was aluf. With the addition of the new rank, aluf became the equivalent of a major general. And Moshe Dayan's rank now translated into English as "lieutenant general." This is why you will see some individuals given different ranks in different documents or other books.

The ranks themselves can be confusing in the military. When I was four years old, my father enlisted for World War II, and was sent to Officers Candidate School. He graduated and became a second lieutenant. Later he was promoted to first lieutenant. Now even a four-year old understood that "first" came before "second." It was puzzling to me then, and neither of my parents could explain to my satisfaction why a new officer didn't become a first lieutenant, and be advanced to second lieutenant. I learned later that this seeming anomaly is because when the ranks were created, lieutenants were viewed rather like deputies to a ship's captain. His "first" lieutenant was his main deputy, and thus the senior in rank to his "second" lieutenant . . .

Of course, the equivalent rank to a Navy captain is not a captain in one of the other services, but rather a colonel in the Army, Navy, or Marine Corps. The equivalent Navy rank to captain in one of those services is first lieutenant. That's just the way it is. The roots of these ranks lie in history.

The "flag officer" equivalent ranks in the U.S. Army, Navy, Marine Corps, and Air Force are as follows:

U.S. ARMY, AIR FORCE, MARINE CORPS	U.S. NAVY
Brigadier General	Commodore (not currently used) or Rear Admiral (lower half)
Major General	Rear Admiral (upper half)
Lieutenant General	Vice Admiral
General	Admiral
General of the Army or Air Force (not used since WW II and no Marine Corps equivalent rank)	Fleet Admiral (not used since WW II)
General of the Armies (used only once . . . for General of the Armies John J. Pershing	

But don't think that ends the discussion, because foreign ranks aren't necessarily equivalent. For example, the U.S. rank, brigadier general, was borrowed from the British. But the Germans and Russians (among others) don't use it. A major general in these armies equals a brigadier general in the U.S. or British armies. A comparison would look like this:

U.S.	GERMAN, RUSSIAN
Brigadier General	Major-General
Major General	Lieutenant-General
Lieutenant General	Colonel-General
General	Field Marshal
General of the Army or Air Force	Marshal

Now, the British also use the rank of Field Marshal, but as an additional complication, the Royal Air Force uses different ranks. Equivalencies look like this:

U.S.	ROYAL AIR FORCE
Brigadier General	Air Commodore
Major General	Air Vice Marshal
Lieutenant General	Air Marshal
General	Air Chief Marshal
General of the Army or Air Force	Marshal of the RAF

But when all is said and done a general or an admiral or the equivalents are the folks who run the show in the military no matter what their titles. So it really doesn't make much difference for our purposes what they are called. During some time I spent flying with the navy, I was sometimes addressed as "admiral" rather than "general" much to the embarrassment of the individual who had addressed me as such as soon as the mistake was recognized. I always found it mildly amusing and would respond with, "Don't apologize, I'm honored. 'Admiral' is an honorable title isn't it?" So no matter what their titles, these are the contributors who learned their wisdom in battle on land, sea, or in the air.

Major General Yigael Allon, **Army of Israel (1918–1980)**

After graduating from agricultural school, Allon joined the Haganah, the underground Jewish Army, during the British occupation of Palestine. He gained his first combat experience during the Arab riots against the Jews in 1936–39 and became an officer. During Israel's War of Independence, in 1948–49, he became a brigadier general while still in his twenties. Allon left the Army due to political differences with David Ben Gurion, Israel's first prime minister. He became a member of Israel's parliament, and held various posts in the Israeli government, including Minister of Labor, Minister of Education and Culture, Foreign Minister and Deputy Prime Minister.

General of the Air Force Henry H. Arnold, U.S. Air Force (1886–1950)

"Hap" Arnold graduated from West Point in 1907 as an infantry officer. After serving two years in the Philippines, he transferred to the aeronautical section of the Signal Corps and earned his pilot's license after instruction from the Wright Brothers. During WW I, he oversaw the army's aviation training school. He became Chief of Staff of the Army Air Corps prior to WW II and served as commander of the renamed U.S. Army Air Forces during the war. Arnold was instrumental in developing and implementing air strategy on all fronts during the war. He was promoted to full general, and several years after his retirement, was promoted to become the first and only General of the Air Force.

Marshal of France Charles Louis de Belle-Isle, French Army (1684–1761)

Belle-Isle was born of the aristocracy. His support of the claims of the Bavarian Holy Roman Emperor Charles VII resulted in France's entry into the War of Austrian Succession in which he participated. The war's loss made him unpopular. However, he conducted a well-organized retreat from Prague in 1742–43 which saved the French army from surrender. He became Minister of War in 1758 and served for three years during the Seven Years War. During this service, he contributed to a major reorganization of the French Army.

General Simón Bolívar, South American Revolutionary (1783–1830)

Known as "El Libertador" he was a revolutionary and statesman as well as a general. He led the revolution of the northern colonies of Spain in South America and through his brilliance, energy, and abilities won many victories. Upper Peru was named Bolivia in his honor and his authoritarian republicanism permanently influenced Latin American politics.

Napoleon Bonaparte, French Emperor (1769–1821)

Napoleon is considered one of the "Great Captains" of history. He rose from an obscure young officer during the French Revolution to one of the most successful generals of the Republic and finally, Emperor of France. He was a military genius who frequently, against superior numbers, destroyed the traditional armies of Europe and united much of Europe under his banner. Eventually, the decisions to occupy Spain and to invade Russia, combined with the adoption of many of his methods by his enemies, led to his defeat and exile, a return, another defeat and his eventual death from natural causes while again in exile.

General of the Army Omar N. Bradley, U.S. Army (1893–1981)

Omar Bradley was commissioned a 2nd Lieutenant in the infantry on graduating from West Point in 1915. He served in various training assignments during World War I and between wars held various training and intermediate command assignments. These culminated in an assignment to the general staff. He was promoted to brigadier general in early 1941. He replaced General George S. Patton in North Africa and was later transferred to England to help plan the invasion of

Europe. He commanded an army during the liberation of France, and was promoted to full general in command of the 12th Army Group for the final operations in Germany. After the war, he succeeded Eisenhower as Army Chief of Staff. He became the first Chairman of the Joint Chiefs of Staff and was promoted to the rank of General of the Army in 1950.

Julius Caesar, Ancient Roman General (100–44 B.C.)

Caesar was born into the aristocracy of Rome. As a young man he served in Asia, and then fought pirates and other enemies of Rome. At the age of 29 he was elected Tribune and entered politics. He served in a number of successively higher military-politico positions including Governor in Spain and then became Proconsul in Gaul. He defeated major tribes in Gaul in numerous campaigns, stopped the German invasion of central Gaul, and invaded Briton. In one famous historical deed, he led his army across the Rubicon and into Italy, an illegal act under Roman law, in order to move against his rival Pompey. He defeated Pompey's forces all over Italy. His success was due not only to his being a brilliant strategist, but his great leadership. It was said that he knew the names of every single one of his legionnaires. He was assassinated by a group of aristocrats on March 15th, 44 B.C.

Major General Joshua L. Chamberlain, U.S. Army (1828–1914)

Joshua Chamberlain was a college professor at Bowdoin College in Maine. When the Civil War broke out, he enlisted in the Union army as a private, and obtained a commission shortly thereafter. By 1863, he was a lieutenant colonel in command of the 20th Maine Volunteers defending Little Round Top at the Battle of Gettysburg. After repeated Confederate attacks, and with ammunition depleted, he ordered a charge with bayonets, which saved the position, and possibly the battle. Gravely wounded in 1864, he was promoted to brigadier general by General Grant on what was thought to be Chamberlain's deathbed. However, he recovered and ended the war as a major general. After the war he returned to Bowdoin, and eventually served as Bowdoin's president and as Governor of Maine. He died of his wounds at age 92.

General Bruce C. Clarke, U.S. Army (1901–1988)

Clarke was commissioned a 2nd lieutenant in the Corps of Engineers after graduating from West Point in 1925. During World War II, he held several important combat commands, and was promoted to brigadier general in 1944 and major general in 1951. He commanded the I and X Corps during and immediately after the Korean War as a lieutenant general, and was promoted to full general in 1958 commanding the U.S. Army Continental Command, and Central Army Group, Allied Forces Europe. After retiring in 1962, he became Vice Chairman of the Freedoms Foundation.

Major General Carl von Clausewitz, Prussian Army (1780–1831)

Clausewitz entered the Prussian army at the age of 12 and was commissioned a year later. He fought in several wars as a young officer and was one of thirty officers who resigned their commissions on the eve of the French invasion of Russia to protest Prussia's status as France's puppet. He served as a staff officer during the War of Liberation against Napoleon and was promoted to major general. He began writing his book, *On War,* in 1819. The book was still incomplete and he was back on active duty during the Polish Revolution in 1830 when he contracted cholera and died. His book, *On War,* was put together from his incomplete manuscripts and published by his wife. *On War* has probably had a greater impact on modern warfare than any other work on the subject.

General Wilbur L. Creech, U.S. Air Force (b 1927)

"Bill" Creech was commissioned a 2nd lieutenant in the Air Force after graduating from flying training in 1949. He flew 103 combat missions as a fighter pilot over North Korea and served a second combat tour as a forward air controller. In 1968, as a colonel he became deputy commander for operations of a fighter wing in Vietnam and flew an additional 174 combat missions. He commanded several fighter wings in Europe and was promoted to brigadier general. He held various posts in research and development as a major general. In 1974 he was promoted to lieutenant general, and in 1978, on assuming command of Tactical Air Command, to full general. He retired in 1982 and was one of the originators of the Total Quality Management concept.

Oliver Cromwell, English Army (1599–1658)

Cromwell graduated from Cambridge and after several years as a rural landowner, was elected to Parliament. With the onset of civil war, he raised a troop of cavalry in rebellion against the throne. As commander of a cavalry regiment, he proved himself exceptionally able and was further promoted. At a major victory at Marston Moor, he led the allied army's left wing of cavalry. When the New Model Army was created, he was appointed second in command and promoted to lieutenant general. He led the army in the Second Civil War and later, as Commander in Chief, led an army to Ireland where he conquered a stronghold and massacred much of the garrison and many civilians. He returned to England to command in the Third Civil War. After destroying the Royalist army, he again led the army in the First Anglo-Dutch War. By then, he had acquired considerable power. He was named Lord Protector. He refused the crown and during one of many periods of haggling with Parliament, caught malaria and died.

Lieutenant General Moshe Dayan, Army of Israel (1915–1981)

Moshe Dayan was born on one of the first Kibbutz (collective farms) founded by Jews in what was then Palestine. While still a teenager, he enlisted in the Haganah, the force formed by Jews to defend against Arab attacks. He fought for the British in their invasion of Vichy Syria and was seriously wounded, losing his left eye in 1941. After the invasion of newly independent Israel by surrounding Arab countries in 1948, he fought against the Syrians in the north, and commanded a jeep-mounted commando battalion. He later commanded the Jerusalem sector and was promoted to what was then the comparable rank of major general and made Chief of Staff of the Israeli Defense Forces in 1953. In this position, he planned and executed the Sinai Campaign against Egypt in 1956. He retired the following year. In the interim years he served in various government posts and went to Vietnam as a correspondent. He became Defense Minister during Israel's Six Day War of 1967 and served in this position during the Yom Kippur War of 1973 as well. He was Foreign Minister during the Camp David Accords which led to peace with Egypt.

Grand Admiral Karl Donitz, German Navy (1891–1980)

Donitz entered the German Navy at the age of 19 and volunteered for the new submarine force in which he served in combat during World War I. He was selected to remain in the Navy after the war, and when the Submarine Force (prohibited by the Versailles Treaty of 1919) was revealed after Hitler's rise to power, he was named its chief. He was promoted to rear admiral commanding all submarines shortly after the start of World War II. He ran a successful campaign in the North Atlantic, but clashed repeatedly with other service chiefs and the commander of the Navy over resource allocations. He was promoted to vice admiral in 1940, and full admiral in 1942. He became commander of the German Navy and Grand Admiral in 1943. Hitler designated Donitz to be Chancellor in his will, and Donitz headed the German government for one week prior to the end of the war. After the war, Donitz was tried and convicted as a war criminal and spent ten years in Spandau prison.

General James "Jimmy" Doolittle, U.S. Air Force (1896–1993)

"Jimmy" Doolittle served as a flight instructor during World War I. Afterwards he achieved many honors including being the first pilot to fly across the U.S. in less than a day and made the first blind instrument landing. He resigned his army commission in 1930. Recalled to active duty just prior to WW II, he led a raid of sixteen B–25 bombers from the aircraft carrier USS Hornet for the first bombing raid on Japan. On his return to the States, he was awarded the Congressional Medal of Honor and promoted to brigadier general. He finished the war as a lieutenant general and returned to civilian life after the war and his pre-war position as an executive with Shell Oil. In 1985, Doolittle was promoted to the rank of full general on the retired list, making him the only reserve officer in U.S. history to be promoted to four star rank.

Major General Giulio Douhet, Italian Air Force (1869–1930)

Douhet was an Italian army officer who early became interested in flying. He commanded the world's first aerial bombardment unit in Libya in 1909. He was made head of the Italian Air Service in 1915, but court-martialed and imprisoned for criticizing army leaders. He was recalled in 1918. In 1921 he wrote his book *The Command of the Air* (*II Dominio dell' Aria*), in which he proclaimed air power as the ultimate offensive weapon. against which there was little defense. He argued for an independent air force. He was the first, and some think the greatest, air power theorist.

Admiral Sir Francis Drake, British Navy (1540–1596)

Drake explored the Americas and was a successful privateer captain during wars against the Spanish. He is best known for defeating the Spanish Armada in 1588, which saved England from defeat.

General Ira C. Eaker, U.S. Air Force (1896–1987)

Eaker graduated from Southeastern State Teachers College in Oklahoma and was commissioned in the Army for World War I. He completed pilot training and was sent to the Philippines. He flew as a pilot for a number of aviation "firsts" between World Wars I and II including the first transcontinental flight made solely on instruments and setting the record for remaining aloft through aerial refueling. As a brigadier general, Eaker took command of the 8th Bomber Command in England and led the first American heavy bomber raid on Europe. When the 8th Bomber Command became the 8th Air Force, he headed it as a major general and advocated daylight precision bombing raids despite the heavy losses the British had had with daylight attacks. He commanded the Mediterranean Allied Air Forces as a lieutenant general, and after the war became deputy commander of the Army Air Forces and chief of the Air Staff. He retired in 1947 as a lieutenant general, but was promoted to full general by Congress prior to his death.

General of the Army Dwight D. Eisenhower, U.S. Army (1890–1969)

Eisenhower graduated from West Point in the class of 1915, approximately in the middle of his class, and was commissioned a 2nd Lieutenant in the infantry. At the outbreak of World War I, he tried unsuccessfully to be assigned to combat duties in France, but his stateside training assignment was considered too important. In 1926, he graduated at the top of his class in Command and General Staff School, and before the war he worked for General MacArthur, when MacArthur was Chief of Staff of the Army, and later as head of the Philippine Army. Back in the States, he was so successful as Third Army Chief of Staff during maneuvers that he skipped the rank of colonel and became a brigadier general in 1941. He commanded the invasion of North Africa, directed the conquest of Tunisia, and commanded the invasions of Sicily and mainland Italy. He was made Supreme Allied Commander of the Allied Expeditionary Force which invaded Europe and defeated Germany. He was promoted to general of the army rank and became Army Chief of Staff. After he retired, he became president of Columbia University, was recalled as the first Supreme Allied Commander, Europe and served as President of the U.S. from 1952 to 1960.

Admiral David G. Farragut, U.S. Navy (1801–1870)

Farragut was appointed a midshipman in the navy at the age of 10. Despite his age, he successfully commanded a prize ship in the Pacific only three years later. He learned Arabic, French, and Italian and was promoted to lieutenant in 1823. He commanded several ships and served against pirates in the Caribbean, off Cuba, South America and other areas. When the Civil War broke out, he was given command of the Western Blockade Force. He captured New Orleans in 1862 and after joint operations with General Grant at Vicksburg, was promoted to rear admiral. Attacking Mobile, Alabama with his forces in 1864, his lead ship struck a mine. He is credited with the famous quote, "Damn the torpedoes, full speed ahead." He was promoted to vice admiral in 1864, and the newly created rank of admiral in 1866.

Field Marshal Ferdinand Foch, French Army (1851–1929)

Foch enlisted for the Franco-Prussian War in 1870 in the infantry. He entered the École Polytechnique and was commissioned a 2nd Lieutenant of artillery on graduation in 1873. He served in a number of command and staff positions until graduating from and then returning to the Senior War College as a professor in 1885. There his concepts on warfare impressed both students and faculty, and resulted in several books. He was promoted to general of brigade in 1907 and given command of a corps six years later. From corps command, he was given command of an army and by 1915, an army group. In 1917, he succeeded General Petain as Chief of the General Staff. He was made the Supreme Allied Commander in the west in 1918 and promoted to Field Marshal. He was appointed President of the Allied Military Committee at Versailles at the end of the war for instituting the armistice and peace terms with Germany.

General Ronald R. Fogleman, U.S. Air Force (b. 1942)

Fogleman was commissioned in the Air Force on graduation from the U.S. Air Force Academy in 1963. His early assignments were as a flying instructor. He flew two combat tours in Vietnam as a fighter pilot, during which he flew 315 combat missions and was wounded. Between combat tours he attended Duke University and earned a masters degree in History and taught this subject at the Air Force Academy. After various fighter command assignments he was promoted to brigadier general in 1985. Three years later he was promoted to major general, and then in 1990 as a lieutenant general, he was sent to Korea, eventually commanding all U.S. Air Forces in Korea. In 1992 he was promoted to full general and commanded simultaneously U.S. Transportation Command and Air Mobility Command, for the first time commanding transport rather than fighter units. Two years later he became Chief of Staff of the U.S. Air Force. He refused to be considered for elevation to Chairman of the Joint Chiefs of Staff. Further, he asked to leave his assignment early, and requested early retirement without the usual ceremony and award of a medal over what he perceived to be an injustice to one of his generals.

Lieutenant General Nathan Bedford Forrest, Confederate States Army (1821–1877)

Forrest was self-educated and before the Civil War was a farmhand, cotton farmer, and slave dealer. He enlisted in the 7th Tennessee Cavalry as a private but, soon after, raised his own cavalry regiment and became its lieutenant colonel. He escaped with his command when his superior surrendered to Grant at Ft. Donelson in 1862. He was seriously wounded at Shiloh and was given a cavalry brigade and promoted to brigadier general on his recovery. He conducted successful cavalry raids, on one occasion capturing an entire enemy brigade and was promoted to major general. In 1864, he captured Ft. Pillow in Tennessee and was blamed for the massacre of black troops attempting to surrender. He conducted numerous raids into areas occupied by union troops, frequently winning against superior odds. He became cavalry commander of the Army of Tennessee and was promoted to lieutenant general in 1865. Forrest was brave and had a natural feel for strategy. He took great pains to take care of his men but was also sometimes brutal and was clearly bigoted. After the war, he was a plantation owner and railroad president. He was a founding member of the Ku Klux Klan, although he later resigned citing its excesses.

Frederick the Great, German Emperor (1712–1786)

Frederick the Great was appointed a colonel in an infantry regiment at the age of 18. He participated in numerous wars, leading the army after he became king following his father's death in 1740. He fought in the First Silesian War, the War of Austrian Succession, the Seven Years War, and the War of Bavarian Succession. His book, *The Instructions of Frederick the Great for His Generals* is frequently quoted and Frederick is celebrated as one of the great captains of history for his tactics and maneuvers which frequently enabled him to win out against superior odds.

Major General Hugo Baron von Freytag-Loringhoven, German Army (1855–1921)

Von Freytag-Loringhoven was born in Copenhagen. He served a few years in the Russian Army before joining the Prussian Guards in 1878. During World War I, he served first as Deputy Chief of Staff of the German Army General Staff's Field Echelon, and later as the Chief of the Army General Staff's Rear Echelon, and Deputy Chief of Staff of the Imperial Army. He is considered one of Germany's foremost military writers. Among his best known books is *The Power of Personality in War.*

General Mikhail V. Frunze, Soviet Army (1885–1925)

Frunze was born into a military family. While studying at the St. Petersburg Polytechnic Institute, he joined the Bolshevik Party and became a full-time revolutionary in 1905. By 1917, he led a Red Guards unit in the Moscow uprising of 1917. When the Russian Civil War broke out, he was rapidly promoted. He successively commanded Red Armies on almost every front as he continually defeated his White Army opponents. After the Civil War, he held a number of political posts culminating as Trotsky's successor as Commissar for Military and

Naval Affairs. He authored several books on war and strategy prior to his death after stomach surgery at the age of 40.

Major General J.F.C. Fuller, **British Army (1878–1964)**

"Boney" Fuller graduated from Sandhurst and was commissioned a 2nd lieutenant in the light infantry in 1898. He fought in South Africa during the Boer War. During World War I he was appointed chief general staff officer of the newly formed Tank Corps and, in this capacity, planned the British tank attack at Cambrai in 1917. The next year he developed the highly innovative Plan 1919 for a combined armored-aerial offensive which was never implemented due to the war's close. After the war, he held a number of senior staff assignments and in 1930 was promoted to major general. However, he had begun writing books, some of which were highly controversial and critical of his superiors. After he published *Generalship: Its Diseases and Their Cure,* he was retired and placed on half-pay. He was briefly associated with British fascists in the early 1930s, but his real career came as he began writing a series of major analytical books on warfare based on his experience and insights.

Lieutenant General Adolf Gallant, **German Air Force (1912–1996)**

"Dolfo" Gallant learned to fly gliders as a teenager, and then entered airline pilot school. He was commissioned a second lieutenant in the German Luftwaffe in 1934 and was assigned to the First Fighter Squadron. He had a serious aircraft accident which nearly cost him his life, and only with great difficulty did he return to flying. He flew with the Condor Legion in Spain from 1937–38, in the Polish Campaign of 1939, the Battle of France in 1940, and in the Battle of Britain. He became a squadron commander and one of Germany's leading aces. In 1941 he became Inspector General of Fighters as a colonel, a year later he was promoted to major general, and later to lieutenant general. He was relieved of this assignment due to differences with Goering and (on his own request) given command of a ME-262 jet fighter squadron. After the war, he worked as an aircraft consultant.

Lieutenant General James M. Gavin, U.S. Army (1907–1990)

"Jumping Jim" Gavin enlisted in the Army in 1924 at the age of seventeen and won an appointment to West Point. Graduating in the class of 1929, he was commissioned in the infantry. In 1941, he became one of the earliest paratroopers. He spearheaded the assault on Sicily as commander of the 505th Parachute Combat Team. As a brigadier general in 1944, he was Eisenhower's advisor on airborne operations. He jumped on D-day in Normandy as assistant commander of the 82nd Airborne Division, which as a major general, he later commanded. As a lieutenant general, he commanded first the VII Corps in Europe after World War II, and then was Army Chief of Research and Development prior to his retirement in 1958. He joined the consulting firm of Arthur D. Little as a vice president, became Ambassador to France from 1961–62, and returned to Arthur D. Little, eventually becoming its Chairman of the Board.

General Ulysses S. Grant, U.S. Army (1822–1885)

"Sam" Grant was born in Ohio and was commissioned a 2nd Lieutenant of Infantry after graduating from West Point in the class of 1843. Two years later he served in the Mexican War, winning two brevet promotions and finishing the war as a brevet captain after participating in the storming of Chapultepec. He received his permanent promotion to captain in 1853, but resigned a year later. As a civilian, he was undistinguished and suffered from alcoholism. When the Civil War started, he was working in his father's dry goods business as a clerk. He was appointed a colonel of the 21st Illinois Volunteer Infantry, and soon thereafter was given command of a District and promoted to brigadier general. He did well, winning battles at Ft. Henry and Ft. Donelson. General Halleck, who was General-in-Chief considered him too aggressive and rash, and he was temporarily relieved of command. After being re-appointed, he was successful at Vicksburg and elsewhere and was promoted to major general in 1863. As the most successful of Union generals, and the only one consistently winning victories, he was made General-in-Chief and promoted to lieutenant general by President Lincoln in 1864. Although he suffered some defeats by Lee, he ultimately prevailed and accepted Lee's surrender at Appomattox Court House on April 9, 1865. He was promoted to full general after the war in 1866. He won two terms as President, but his presidency was marred by corruption. While not personally involved, he was overly trustful of friends; a trait that led him to bankruptcy later. He wrote his memoirs to provide for his family, and completed them only days before his death from throat cancer.

Major General Nathanael Greene, Continental Army (1742–1786)

Greene was born a Quaker, but rebelled against his faith and raised a militia company in 1774. However, the company refused to elect him as captain due to his lame leg, so he served as a private. However, his leadership was recognized and he was appointed a brigadier general of militia and then in the Continental Army the following year. His courage and logistical talents were evident at the Battle of Boston. In 1776, he was appointed major general. He made a poor decision in recommending the retention of Ft. Washington, but his tactical errors were more than offset by his strategic understanding and logistical talents. In 1777, he was appointed quartermaster general and afterwards commanded in major battles in the Southern Colonies. Despite three tactical defeats by the British, he achieved his strategic goals. After the war's end in 1781, he retired to his Savannah, Georgia estate and died five years later.

Brigadier General Samuel B. Griffith, II, U.S. Marine Corps (1903–1983)

Griffith served in the Marine Corps for twenty-five years, and was Commanding Officer of the Marine Corps First Raiders on Guadalcanal and in the New Georgia campaign. During his service, he served in China, Nicaragua, and Cuba as well as Europe and England. He earned both the Navy Cross and the Army's Distinguished Service Cross and held a PhD in Chinese history from Oxford. His scholarship resulted in several books, including one of the most familiar translations of the writings of Sun Tzu.

Colonel General Heinz Guderian, German Army (1888–1953)

After cadet school, Guderian was commissioned a 2nd lieutenant in 1908. During World War I, he served in signals, in various staff assignments, and on the General Staff. After the war, he participated in Free Korps operations in Latvia, and was selected as one of the few officers remaining in the Reichswehr after the war. Before World War II, he became involved in motor transport duties, leading eventually to involvement in the infant tank forces by the early 1930s. He commanded the 2nd Panzer Division and was promoted to major general in 1936. He attained corps command, and participated or led every armored operation in the early stages of the war including the Austrian Anschluss in 1938, the Polish campaign in 1939, the invasion of France in 1940, and the invasion of the U.S.S.R. in 1941. He was relieved of command during the Russian campaign, for repeatedly requesting permission to withdraw his forces from an exposed position. He was recalled to duty as Inspector General of Panzer forces in 1943 and is credited with rebuilding the German armored forces after the defeat at Stalingrad. He became Army Chief of Staff in July of that year. Hitler fired him in 1945 just prior to the war's end.

General Sir John Hackett, British Army (1910–1997)

Hackett was born in Western Australia and attended Oxford. He was commissioned into the 8th Hussars at the age of 21. Prior to World War II, he served in what was then Palestine. During the war, he served in Syria, the Western Desert, and Italy and was wounded twice. In 1944, he commanded a parachute brigade as a brigadier general. At the Battle of Arnhem, he was badly wounded a third time and was hidden by a Dutch family for four months until well enough to travel and escape by bicycle. After the war, he held senior appointments including Commander-in-Chief, British Army of the Rhine and Commander, Northern Army Group, NATO. After retirement, he served as Principal of King's College, London from 1968–1975.

Admiral William F. Halsey, U.S. Navy (1882–1959)

"Bull" Halsey graduated from Annapolis in the class of 1904 and spent most of his early career in destroyers and torpedo boats, including convoy escort duty during World War I. After the war, he served on destroyers in both the Atlantic and the Pacific. He was promoted to the rank of captain in 1927. He completed naval pilot training at the age of 52 in 1935 and was promoted to rear admiral and commanded a carrier division shortly thereafter. Just prior to World War II, he was promoted to vice admiral. After the war broke out, he raided several Japanese islands. He was promoted to admiral, commanded the South Pacific area and went on to capture the Solomon Islands from the Japanese. He commanded the Third Fleet in its major battle with the Japanese fleet and was promoted to fleet admiral at the end of the war.

General Sir Ian Hamilton, British Army (1853–1947)

Hamilton joined the British Army at the age of 19 and fought in a number of colonial wars. These included the Second Afghan War

(1878 to 1880), the First and Second Boer Wars (1891 and 1899 to 1902), the Mahdist War (1883 to 1898), the Third Burmese War (1885 to 1886) and the Tirah Campaign (1897 to 1898). He commanded a brigade as a colonel during this campaign and was appointed lieutenant general during the Second Boer War. Returning to England, he became Quartermaster General. During World War I, he directed the landings at Gallipoli, and afterwards published several books on the campaigns in which he participated.

Hannibal, Ancient Carthaginian General (247–183 B.C.)

Hannibal was a Carthaginian general, the son of Hamilcar Barca, commander of Carthaginian forces during the first Punic War with Rome. Hannibal became commander of the cavalry in the army of his older brother Hasdrubal. After Hasdrubal's assassination, he took over command of the whole army. He initiated an invasion of the Italian homeland which began the Second Punic War. However, since Rome controlled the Mediterranean, he traveled overland through Spain and eventually crossed the Alps. He defeated one Roman Army after another, the most famous of which was the battle of Cannae in 216 B.C. in which he faced an army under the Roman general Varro more than four times his army's size. Employing a controlled withdrawal of his lightly defended center, with his main forces concentrated on his flanks, he performed a double envelopment of Roman forces. It was the most decisive battle in the history of warfare, with 80% of the Roman force left dead on the battlefield. Despite his continuous victories, he was not supported by Carthage sufficiently to defeat Rome. He was recalled to defend the homeland, when the Romans developed a strategy to draw him off, and he was defeated by the Roman general Scipio. After the peace he was forced to flee. He poisoned himself to avoid capture saying, "Let us release the Romans from their long anxiety, since they think it too long to wait for the death of an old man."

Field Marshal Paul von Hindenburg, German Army (1847–1934)

Von Hindenburg entered the Royal Cadet Corps and was commissioned a 1st lieutenant six years later in 1866. He was in combat first in the Seven Weeks War in 1866. He fought again in the Franco-Prussian War of 1870–1871. Six years later, he became a member of the General Staff. By 1889, he was a general and a corps commander. In 1911, he retired. However, when Germany went to war in 1914, he was recalled to command the Eighth Army in Prussia. Winning major victories against the Russians, he was appointed commander of Austro-German forces on the Eastern front and promoted to Field Marshal. In 1916, he became Chief of the General Staff. He was relieved of duties three weeks before the armistice ending World War I in 1918. In 1925, he was elected President of the Weimar Republic.

Major General Andrew Jackson, U.S. Army (1767–1845)

"Old Hickory" served first during the Revolutionary war, during which he was captured by the British and while a prisoner was saber-slashed by a drunken British officer. After the war, he studied and practiced law, served as Tennessee's first Congressman and was elected to the Senate. In 1802 he became a major general in the Tennessee state militia. When the War of 1812 broke out with Britain, his troops went into government service. He prepared to invade Florida, but the operation was cancelled the last minute leaving his troops stranded in Mississippi with no pay, food, or transport. Despite this, he maintained discipline and led his force back to Tennessee. He conducted several successful campaigns against the Creek Indians who were allied with the British and was named a major general in the Regular Army. In 1815, he successfully defended New Orleans against British attack, the only major American land success of the war. After the war, he received command of the Southern Division, and he led forces successfully in the First

Seminole War of 1817–1818. When the army was reduced after this war, he resigned his commission. He served as U.S. President from 1828 to 1836.

Lieutenant General Thomas Jackson, **Confederate States Army (1824–1863)**

"Stonewall" Jackson was commissioned a 2nd lieutenant of artillery after graduating from West Point in the class of 1846. He fought in the Mexican War and won distinction at Veracruz and Chapultepec. He was breveted to the rank of major. He resigned his commission and taught artillery and natural philosophy at the Virginia Military Institute. Interestingly, he was not well liked by the cadets who called him "Tom Fool" Jackson. When the Civil War came, he was commissioned a colonel and promoted to brigadier general a couple months later. His solid defense of a strategic hill at the First Battle of Bull Run gained him the nickname "Stonewall." A month later he was promoted to major general and put in command of all forces in the Shenandoah Valley where he out-maneuvered and defeated Union forces several times his size. He was promoted to lieutenant general in October of 1862, and given command of II Corps. At Chancellorsville in May of 1863, his corps made a major contribution to the Confederate victory. However, he was mistakenly shot by one of his own men. His left arm was amputated and he contracted pneumonia and died a week later.

Joan of Arc, **French Army (1412–1431)**

"The Maid of Orleans" heard what she believed to be voices from God directing her to take up the cause of the Dauphin, Charles against the English Invasion during the Hundred Years War. She gained an audience with the Dauphin and due to a combination of her zeal and his desperation (he had tried just about everything else), he was advised to agree to her demands. He gave this untrained, 18-year old girl command of the French Army. She immediately undertook to raise the siege of Orleans which the French had tried to do unsuccessfully for eight months. Under Joan's leadership, the French army accomplished this feat in just eight days. She then took Reims so that Charles could be crowned there as king. In the process, she destroyed the English Army. Some months later she set out to relieve the city of Compiegne, but was captured. She was tried by representatives of the Catholic Church and convicted of heresy. She admitted her heresy in exchange for the sentence of abandonment to secular authority. She was therefore retried by the English who sentenced her to permanent imprisonment. However, she renounced her earlier admission of heresy and was burned at the stake the next day. She was canonized by Pope Benedict XV in 1920.

General Henri de Jomini, **French Army, Russian Army (1779–1869)**

Jomini was born in Switzerland and started his career as a banker in 1796, first in Basel, and then Paris. He returned to Switzerland to work in the war ministry when the Swiss Republic was declared. He became a major, returned to Paris, and began to write about war. French Marshal Ney read his book and helped him to publish it. He joined Ney's staff. After reading the book, Napoleon promoted him to colonel and he served on Napoleon's staff. He served on the staff of Ney again in several capacities including Chief of Staff and was promoted to brigadier general. During the Russian campaign he served as Military Governor of Vilno and later Smolensk. He was recommended for promotion to major general by Ney, but before this could occur, his enemy Marshal Berthier had him arrested on somewhat dubious charges. Incensed, he deserted to the Russian Army and was made a lieutenant general. Napoleon later said that his desertion was justified. Desertion and switching of sides was considered acceptable in those times, so long as this change in allegiance did not involve treason. During the war with Turkey (1828–1829), he was promoted to full general by Czar Nicholas I. He published his most famous book, *The Art of War* in 1838, and retired after the Crimean War in 1859.

Rear Admiral John Paul Jones, Continental Navy, Russian Navy (1747–1792)

Jones was born in Scotland with the family name Paul. He went to sea on a merchant ship as a cabin boy at the age of 12. He took command of his first ship seven years later when both captain and chief mate died at sea. He was charged with killing a mutinous sailor in 1773. Rather than stand trial, he changed his name to Jones and fled to America, where he had a brother. In 1775 he was commissioned senior lieutenant in the Continental Navy. During the War of Independence he commanded several ships of war and sank and captured numerous enemy ships. Eventually he was given command of the *America* with 74 guns. After the war, he was the only naval officer to receive a Congressional Gold Medal for his services. With the draw down of the Continental Navy, he accepted a commission in the Russian Navy as a Rear Admiral and defeated the Turks at the Battle of Liman. He left Russian service suffering from ill health and died in Paris. His remains were brought to the U.S. and he was buried at the U.S. Naval Academy in 1913.

Genghis Khan, Mongol General (1162–1227)

Genghis Khan was the heir to the head of a subclan of a major Mongol tribe. However, when his father was poisoned, the throne was claimed by a cousin, and Genghis was driven into exile in the desert. Two years later, at the age of 17, he led a raid to capture his kidnapped bride. His military skill was soon apparent, and leading an army of 20,000, he repulsed an attack by his cousin leading a larger force. Genghis defeated, captured, and executed him. With a genius for organization and discipline, he reorganized the Mongols and his superior organization soon won numerous victories. He declared himself the Supreme War Emperor in 1205 and conquered Mongolia and most of China. He invaded and conquered land in Persia and India, and Afghanistan, organizing his army of 200,000 into four hordes, each approximating a modern corps. At the time of his death from illness, units of his army had conquered parts of Russia.

Admiral of the Fleet Ernest J. King, U.S. Navy (1878–1956)

"Rey" King was commissioned an ensign after graduating from the U.S. Naval Academy in 1901. However, while still a midshipman, he had already served on the U.S.S. San Francisco during the Spanish American War. During World War I, he served in the Atlantic Fleet and was promoted to captain. In the early 1920s, he took submarine training and commanded Submarine Division 11. At the age of 48, he took pilot training and received his wings. After a number of aviation commands, he was promoted to rear admiral and in 1933 became Chief of the Bureau of Aeronautics. Five years later, he was promoted to vice admiral and put in command of a five-carrier Aircraft Battle Force. In early 1941, he was promoted to full admiral and given command of the Atlantic Fleet during which period he directed the anti-submarine war against Germany even before U.S. entry into the war. As Commander-in-Chief, U.S. Fleet from 1942 on, he played a major role in naval strategy throughout the war. He was promoted to Fleet Admiral in 1944. After retiring in 1945 he served as advisor to Secretaries of the Navy, and the President until his death.

Major General Henry Knox, Continental Army (1750–1806)

Knox joined the militia at the age of 18 and the Continental Army seven years later. He fought at Bunker Hill and was promoted to colonel in the Regiment of Artillery. Washington sent him to retrieve the artillery captured at Ft. Ticonderoga, which he did, bringing 66 pieces over 300 miles in the middle of winter snow. This artillery assisted in several important American victories. After the victory at Trenton, Knox was promoted to brigadier general. He established arsenals and an artillery school, and is considered the "father" of American artillery development. In 1782, Knox was promoted to major general, retroactive to 1781, making him the youngest major general in American forces. In 1782, he succeeded Washington as Commander-in-Chief. He served as Secretary of War from 1785 to 1794 including serving as the first U.S. Secretary of War under Washington from 1789. He died an accidental death choking on a chicken bone.

General Robert E. Lee, Confederate States Army (1807–1870)

"Uncle Robert" Lee graduated from West Point in the class of 1829 and was commissioned a 2nd lieutenant in the Corps of Engineers. He served with distinction during the War with Mexico, and it was his reconnaissance which found the route for General Scott's flanking force which overcame Mexican resistance. He was awarded three brevet promotions for his services. He was Superintendent of the U.S. Military Academy for three years (1852–55), and than transferred to the cavalry. As colonel, he commanded the 2nd Cavalry Regiment in Texas, and was in command of the operations which captured John Brown at Harper's Ferry in 1860. As the Civil War loomed, he was the leading candidate to become General-in-Chief of Federal forces. He was not a champion of slavery, and he opposed secession. Nevertheless, when his state, Virginia, seceded from the Union, he resigned his commission saying, "I cannot draw my sword against my friends and neighbors." He was given command of Virginia's military forces and when these forces were incorporated into the Confederate Army, Lee became military advisor to President Jefferson Davis. He did poorly in his first field command, but when General Joseph Johnston was wounded, he replaced him as commander of what became the Army of Northern Virginia. Lee's accomplishments over the next three years were extraordinary. Fighting always against superior numbers, and with insufficient supplies and food, he beat his opponents again and again. Only at the end, did this superiority, in the competent hands of generals such as Grant, win out. Three months before the war ended he was made General-in-Chief of Confederate forces. After the war, he resisted all attempts of Northern and Southern companies alike to make use of his name in business deals, but accepted the presidency of a small college which has since become Washington and Lee University.

Lieutenant General John A. Lejeune, U.S. Marine Corps (1867–1942)

As a "passed midshipman" at the United States Naval Academy, Lejeune served on the Cruiser Vandalia which sank during a storm. Lejeune graduated and was commissioned a 2nd lieutenant in the Marine Corps. He served on ship during the blockade of Cuba in 1898 and as a battalion commander, landed at Panama in 1904. He was the first Marine officer to attend and graduate from the Army War College in 1910. In 1913, Lejeune was put in command of the Mobile Regiment and as a colonel in 1914, he served as acting brigade commander at Vera Cruz. In 1917, he was promoted to brigadier general and given command of the Army's 64th brigade in France. He became commander of the 2nd Division, and in 1918 he was promoted to major general, becoming the first Marine to command a U.S. Army division. As such, he won a series of victories in France during World War I. He became Commandant of the Marine Corps in 1920 and served until 1929 when he retired and became the Superintendent of The Virginia Military Institute. He retired in 1937 at age 70 and was promoted to lieutenant general just prior to his death in 1942.

General Curtis E. LeMay (1906–1990)

Curtis LeMay attended Ohio State University and after Aviation Cadet Training was commissioned a 2nd lieutenant in the Army Air Corps in 1930. As a B-17 navigator and pilot, he participated in several record-breaking flights prior to WW II. He was promoted to captain and given command of a squadron in 1940. As a colonel he commanded the 305th Bombardment Group in England in late 1942 and 1943. He was then promoted to brigadier general and in 1944, to major general and transferred to China. Later, he became commander of the 21st Bomb Group on Guam in operations against the Japanese. After the war, he was promoted to lieutenant general and then given command of U.S. Air Forces in Europe. He planned and ran the Berlin airlift against the Soviet blockade of that city in 1948. The following year he was promoted and became the youngest full general since Ulysses S. Grant. He became commander of the Strategic Air Command then became Air Force Chief of Staff in 1961. He clashed with Secretary of Defense Robert S. McNamara repeatedly, and recent historians have credited him with being the foremost head-of-service opponent to the administration's strategies in Vietnam. He retired in 1965, and ran unsuccessfully as a vice presidential candidate in 1968.

General of the Army Douglas MacArthur, U.S. Army (1880–1964)

MacArthur was commissioned a 2nd lieutenant of engineers after graduating from West Point in 1903. He was assigned as an aide to his father General Arthur MacArthur in the Philippines. Three years later he served as an aide to President Theodore Roosevelt, and later on the General Staff. MacArthur took part in the Vera Cruz campaign of 1914. When America entered World War I, he was granted a commission as a colonel in the infantry. In 1918 he was promoted to brigadier general and became a divisional commander. After the war MacArthur served as Superintendent of West Point. He was promoted to major general, commanded the Department of the Philippines and skipped the rank of lieutenant general to become a full general and Army Chief of Staff from 1930 to 1935. He reverted to major general and was sent to the Philippines to organize its defenses. He retired there in 1936 and was named a Field Marshal by the Philippine Government. In 1941, he was recalled to the U.S. Army as a lieutenant general. After the Japanese invasion, he was evacuated on orders of President Roosevelt and made Supreme Allied Commander of Allied Forces in the Southwest Pacific. He recaptured the Philippines in 1944, once again a full general. He was promoted to General of the Army shortly before Japan surrendered. He served as Supreme Commander of Allied occupation forces in Japan until named Supreme Commander of U.N. forces in Korea. Despite a brilliant performance in this role, he was relieved of his duties by President Truman due to strong disagreements and what was perceived as insubordination. MacArthur retired from the Army a second time in 1951.

Field Marshal Gustav von Mannerheim, Finnish Army (1867–1951)

After a military education, Mannerheim was commissioned a 2nd lieutenant of cavalry in the Russian Army in 1889. He saw action in the Russo-Japanese war of 1905 and soon after was a colonel. During World War I, Mannerheim became a lieutenant general and Corps Commander. However, after the Russian Revolution, he returned to his homeland to command anti-Communist forces. He became Regent of Finland until a republic was declared in 1920. He retired, but returned to government service in 1931 and was made Chairman of the Defense Council. When the USSR invaded Finland in 1939, Mannerheim was made Commander-in-Chief. He fought the Russians until forced to surrender in 1940. When war resumed the following year, he again took command. He was made a Field Marshal in 1942, and elected President of Finland two years later.

Mao Tse-tung, Head of Chinese Revolutionary Army (1893–1976)

Mao was born of a well-to-do peasant and landowner family. He received an excellent education, becoming a teacher and a leading intellectual. He was a founding member of the Chinese Communist Party (CCP) in 1921. In 1927, Mao formed a revolutionary army without official CCP sanction and led an abortive uprising. His only previous military experience had been as an orderly in a militia unit during the Chinese Revolution of 1911. He was severely criticized and fired from the CCP politboro by the party leadership. However, he maintained control of his forces and fled to the mountains, eventually governing about 15 million people there. Mao gained control of CCP forces in 1935, and moved with them to a new base 6,000 miles away. Only 4,000 of 86,000 arrived a year later. This is referred to as "The Long March." During World War II, he formed a united front with the Kuomintang against the Japanese. After World War II, he drove the Kuomintang out of China during the Civil War of 1946–1947, proclaimed the Peoples Republic of China, and intervened militarily against the U.S. and United Nations forces to maintain Communist domination of North Korea. He retired as Chief of State in 1958, but continued to exercise considerable influence, including opening relations with the U.S. in 1972.

General of the Army George C. Marshall, U.S. Army (1880–1959)

Marshall graduated from the Virginia Military Institute in 1901 and was commissioned a 2nd lieutenant of Infantry a year later. He served in combat in the Philippines and later in France as a senior staff officer and a colonel during World War I but after the war reverted to the rank of captain. He was promoted to major in 1920 and lieutenant colonel in 1923. He became a colonel in 1933 and a brigade commander and brigadier general three years later. In 1938, he was appointed head of the War Plans Division, and became a major general. Later in the year, he became deputy chief of staff and then as a full general, Chief of Staff of the Army. He built the Army from 200,000 to its wartime strength of 8,000,000. He was promoted to the rank of General of the Army in 1944. A speech he made calling for economic aid to reconstruct Europe led to the Marshall Plan. He became Secretary of State in 1947, and Secretary of Defense in 1950. He was the first military man to be awarded the Nobel Prize for Peace.

Brigadier General S.L.A. Marshall, U.S. Army (1901–1977)

"SLAM" Marshall enlisted in the Army for World War I. He won a battlefield commission as a 2nd lieutenant of Infantry at the age of 17, the youngest officer in the American Expeditionary Force. After the war he resigned from the Army. Between wars, he worked as a reporter and attended the Texas College of Mines, now the University of Texas at El Paso. He worked as a war correspondent in Central and South America, Spain and Europe and wrote several books on warfare. When war came, he served first as a consultant to the Secretary of War, and then in the Special Service Division of the General Staff. By 1943, he was a lieutenant colonel visiting and conducting personal interview surveys after the battles on all fronts. He originated a unique idea in writing history: he interviewed as many members as possible of a unit as soon after the battle as possible, and using these interviews as a basis, wrote a history of the battle or campaign. In 1944, he was promoted to colonel. Although he again left the Army after World War II, he retained a reserve commission, and in various capacities, traveled to Korea, the Congo, and the Middle East, interviewing, writing histories, and analyzing battles. He was promoted to brigadier general in

1953. Although he retired from the Army in 1958, he continued to perform this function in a civilian capacity.

Rear Admiral Alfred Thayer Mahan, U.S. Navy (1840–1914)

For an admiral and naval strategist, Mahan had an unusual distinction: he was born at West Point; his father having been a well-known military thinker and writer, and a professor there at the time. Mahan graduated from Annapolis in the class of 1859. He performed blockade duty during the Civil War and was promoted to lieutenant commander at the war's end. Mahan was promoted to commander in 1872 and captain in 1885. He taught and eventually served as president of the Naval War College, afterwards writing several books, among them *The Influence of Sea Power upon History, 1660–1783,* his most famous work. He commanded the steel cruiser Chicago on a European cruise and retired shortly thereafter in 1896. He was recalled to serve on the Naval War Board during the Spanish-American War in 1898, and was delegate to the peace conference at The Hague in 1899. Mahan became president of the American Historical Association in 1902 and was promoted to rear admiral while on the retired list in 1906.

Major General F. W. von Mellenthin, German Army (b. 1904)

Von Mellenthin was born into a military family. His father was killed in action during World War I. After graduating from high school in 1924, he enlisted in the cavalry. In 1926, he attended both infantry and cavalry schools, and was commissioned a lieutenant in 1928. In 1935, von Mellenthin was sent to the War Academy in Berlin for training as a General Staff officer. In 1937, he was appointed to the staff of the III Corps as a captain. He served during the Polish Campaign as a major and as Rommel's Chief of Staff, in North Africa, and later as a colonel and Chief of Staff for the 48th Panzer Corps, Fourth Panzer Army, and as major general, Chief of Staff of Army Group G, West. After the war, he immigrated to South Africa and wrote a number of military books, probably the best known of which is *Panzer Battles.*

Field Marshal Karl Helmuth von Molke, German Army (1800–1891)

Von Molke was educated in the Royal Cadet Corps in Copenhagen and was commissioned into a Danish infantry regiment on graduation. After a visit to Berlin, he decided to become a Prussian officer and was commissioned a lieutenant in the Leibgrenadier Regiment. He joined the General Staff and was sent to Turkey and he fought and distinguished himself in the Turko-Egyptian War of 1838–41. He rejoined the General Staff and in 1857 was made Chief of Staff. Von Molke's appreciation of the importance of railroads and telegraphy plus his reorganization of the general staff led to considerable increase in power, and his work during the Franco-Prussian War of 1870–71 led to promotion to the rank of field marshal.

Field Marshal Bernard L. Montgomery, British Army (1887–1976)

Montgomery graduated from Sandhurst in 1908 and was commissioned in the Royal Warwickshire Regiment. He fought in France in World War I and was badly wounded. Between the wars, his duty included two tours in the Middle East, including one as a divisional commander in Jerusalem. In World War II, he commanded a division in France including commanding the rearguard during the retreat at Dunkerque. He was promoted to corps command and then commanded the 8th Army in Egypt, first repulsing, and than beating Rommel at the Battle of El Alamein. After the campaign in Sicily, he was recalled to Britain to command the Twenty-First Army Group for the invasion of France. After the land battle in Normandy, he was promoted to Field Marshal. In the post war period, he became Chief of the Imperial General Staff and eventually Commander of NATO forces in Europe and deputy Supreme Commander to General Eisenhower.

Admiral Lord Horatio Nelson, Royal Navy (1758–1805)

Nelson entered the British Navy as a midshipman on his uncle's ship at the age of 12. He served on voyages from the West Indies to the Arctic. He was given his first command in 1779 and he commanded several frigates in combat from the West Indies to operations off of Nicaragua. Nelson was placed on half pay from 1787 to 1793, but was recalled when war broke out with France and given command of the 64-gun H.M.S. Agamemnon in the Mediterranean. He lost his right eye in battle in 1794. Nelson was promoted to the rank of Commodore in 1797 and blocked the escape of the Spanish fleet which was allied with the French. He was wounded and lost his right arm the same year. He was promoted to rear admiral and knighted. In 1801 he was promoted to vice admiral and fought as second in command at the battle of Copenhagen. When ordered to discontinue action, he placed a telescope to his blind eye and remarked that he saw no such signal. After war with France was resumed in 1803, he was given command of the Mediterranean fleet. Nelson caught and engaged the French fleet off Trafalgar in 1805 where he sent his famous signal, "England expects every man to do his duty." He won the battle, but lost his life, wounded mortally by a French sharpshooter.

Major General Aubrey Newman, U.S. Army (1903–1994)

"Red" Newman was commissioned a 2nd lieutenant of Infantry after graduating from West Point in 1925. His assignments before World War II included infantry assignments at Ft. Riley, Kansas, and Schofield Barracks Hawaii. When World War II came, he was assigned to the 24th Infantry Division as colonel, serving in a number of positions including that of Chief of Staff. He became a regimental commander in 1944, and made the landing on Red Beach at Leyte in the Philippines. In this action, noting his men stalled on the beach, and despite heavy fire, he stood up and got his regiment moving shouting: "Get the hell off the beach! God damn it, get up and get moving— Follow me!" He was immortalized in an Army poster for this action with a somewhat more refined quotation attributed to him. In 1952, Aubrey became a brigadier general and assistant division commander of the 82nd Airborne Division. He was promoted to major general in 1954 and served in a number of staff positions, retiring in 1960. After retirement, he became a military writer, authoring several books, and as a staff writer for *Army* magazine.

Rear Admiral Richard H. O'Kane, U.S. Navy (1911–1994)

O'Kane was commissioned an ensign after graduating from the U.S. Naval Academy in 1934. He served on several surface ships before completing submarine school in 1938. He served on the USS Argonaut until reporting for duty as executive officer of the USS Wahoo and made several war patrols, sinking numerous enemy ships in this capacity. In 1943, he assumed command of the USS Tang. Tang made five war patrols with O'Kane as captain, sinking 31 ships, the top score of any American submarine. On its fifth patrol Tang was sunk by one of its own torpedoes, which was defective. O'Kane, then a commander was captured by the Japanese. He was awarded the Congressional Medal of Honor and three Navy Crosses for his exploits while in command of the Tang. After the war, O'Kane held several additional ship commands. Promoted first to captain, and then admiral, he commanded submarine school, Submarine Division Thirty-Two and Submarine Squadron Seven. He retired in 1965 and wrote several books about his exploits.

General Alexander M. Patch, U.S. Army (1889–1945)

Patch graduated in the class of 1913 from West Point and was commissioned a 2nd lieutenant of infantry. He served on the Mexican border and then was sent to France as a captain. He ran the Army Machine Gun School and participated in three major combat campaigns, finishing the war as a lieutenant colonel. After the war, he reverted to the rank of captain. He helped develop the triangular organization the army used during World War II, just prior to which, he was promoted to brigadier general. As a major general he led the Americal Division which relieved the 1st Marine Division on Guadalcanal. He took command of the IV Corps in training in the States, and then the 7th Army in Italy, which he commanded through difficult fighting throughout Southern Europe and into France, Germany and Austria. Promoted to full general, he commanded the 4th Army in the States and was named to a special study group for postwar reorganization. He caught pneumonia and died shortly after the study was completed.

General George S. Patton, Jr., U.S. Army (1885–1945)

"Georgie" Patton attended the Virginia Military Institute for a year before going to West Point. He graduated in the class of 1909 and was commissioned in the cavalry after taking five years to complete the four year course. He competed in the 1912 Olympics in Stockholm on the U.S. pentathlon team, and designed an improved cavalry saber. He was with General Pershing's expedition to capture Pancho Villa in Mexico in 1917 and went to Europe with Pershing the same year. He led the 1st Tank Brigade in combat and was slightly wounded. At the age of 29, he was a colonel. After the war, he reverted to the rank of captain and served in cavalry units between wars. He was also a distinguished graduate of the Army's Command and General Staff School. He was promoted to brigadier general in 1940 and major general after being given command of the 2nd Armor Division. Patton was promoted to lieutenant general and given command of the I Armored Corps which became the Seventh Army. He led this unit so well during the Sicilian Campaign that he was clearly destined for greater things . . . it was thought an Army Group for the invasion of Europe. But due to the much-publicized incident of slapping a wounded soldier, he was sent to England and given command of another Army, the Third Army. He led the Third Army across Europe, relieved Bastogne during the German's Ardennes offensive, and crossed the Rhine and pressed into Germany. He was promoted to full general. After the war, his outspoken opposition to de-Nazification got him relieved of command of the Third Army. He was severely injured in an automobile accident and died several weeks later.

General of the Armies John J. Pershing (1860–1948)

"Black Jack" Pershing graduated from West Point in 1886 and was commissioned in the cavalry. He served in several campaigns against the Indians, and got his nickname while serving with the famed 10th Cavalry Regiment "Buffalo Soldiers." He served in the Philippines and was an observer during the Russo-Japanese War of 1905. President Theodore Roosevelt promoted him from captain to brigadier general in 1906 jumping him over 862 more senior officers. Under directions of President Wilson, he led an unsuccessful ten-month invasion of Mexico in 1916 to catch Mexican General Pancho Villa after the later attacked the town of Columbus, New Mexico. He was appointed Commander of the American Expeditionary Force (AEF) in 1917. Despite tremendous pressures, he preserved the AEF as an independent force and directed three major, and successful offensives during World War I. On his return from France he was promoted to the rank of General of the Armies, the only officer ever to have held this or equivalent rank. He served as Chief of Staff from 1921–24.

Philip of Macedonia, Ancient Macedonia Ruler (383–336 B.C.)

During three years as a hostage in Thebes Philip learned warfare from Epaminodas the greatest Thebian general of his age. After his return to Macedon, at age 27, he was proclaimed king. He organized the army and fought at its head, losing an eye in battle. He was successful in various wars against other Greek states, and eventually was named head of a Greek alliance in a formal war against Persia. Philip launched an advanced invasion force of 10,000 troops into Asia, but before he could bring up the rest of the army, he was murdered. The army, led by his son, Alexander the Great, was founded and organized by Philip.

General Colin Powell, U.S. Army (b. 1937)

Colin Powell was commissioned a second lieutenant in the infantry after graduating from the ROTC program at the City College of New York in 1958. He served in Germany, and then in Vietnam in 1962–63 as an advisor to a Vietnamese battalion. He returned to Vietnam after graduating from the Command and General Staff College and served as an infantry battalion executive officer and assistant divisional chief of staff. He was selected as a White House Fellow on his return. Promoted to lieutenant colonel, he commanded a battalion in Korea. After graduating from National War College, he was promoted to colonel and commanded a brigade in the 101st Airborne (Air Assault) Division. He returned to Washington, D.C. and served in a number of senior posts. Powell became assistant division commander of the 4th Mechanized Infantry Division on his promotion to brigadier general. Back in Washington, he became senior military advisor to the Secretary of Defense and was promoted to major general. In 1986, he was promoted to lieutenant general and commanded V Corps in Germany. The following year, Powell returned to Washington again, as assistant for National Security Affairs initially to President Reagan and then President Bush. In 1989, he was named Chairman of the Joint Chiefs of Staff and promoted to full general. In this capacity, he had major responsibilities in the operations against Panama and in Operations Desert Shield and Desert Storm. He retired in 1993, and has served in various capacities supporting community service since. He has refused several attempts to persuade him to run for President.

Lieutenant General Lewis Puller, U.S. Marine Corps (1898–1971)

"Chesty" Puller dropped out of the Virginia Military Institute to enlist in the Marine Corps for World War I in 1917. The war was over before he could get to France, but he was sent to Officers Training school and was commissioned a 2nd lieutenant in the Marine Corps in June of 1919. But two weeks later, Puller was discharged. Seeking action, he went to Haiti and was commissioned in the constabulary under Marine Corps control. As a Marine, he served with distinction in expeditionary campaigns in Nicaragua and China and five campaigns in the Pacific. He retired as a colonel and was almost immediately recalled for the Korean War. Puller's performance was such, especially during the retreat from the Chosin Reservoir after the Chinese entrance into the war, that he was promoted to brigadier general. He was eventually promoted to major general and lieutenant general and retired at the age of 57. He was the most decorated Marine in U.S. history, and the only one to have won five Navy Crosses.

Admiral Hyman Rickover, U.S. Navy (1900–1986)

Rickover was born in Makow, Russia (now Poland). His family emigrated to the U.S. in 1906. He was commissioned an ensign after graduating from the U.S. Naval Academy in 1922. After several tours of sea duty, he was sent to Columbia University where he earned an MS in electrical engineering. Rickover qualified for submarine duty in 1929 and served aboard the submarines S-9 and S-48. In 1937 he was given command of the USS Finch. The same year he was selected as an Engineering Duty Officer and spent the remainder of his career in that specialty. During World War II, he was Head of the Electrical Section of the Bureau of Ships and later Commanding officer of the Naval Repair Base on Okinawa. After the war, Rickover was assigned to the Atomic Energy commission. As director of the Naval Reactors Branch he developed the world's first nuclear powered submarine, the USS Nautilus, launched in 1955. His outspoken advocacy of nuclear power had made him many enemies in the Navy, however, and it was only through Congressional intervention that he was promoted to admiral. Thereafter, Rickover controlled much that went on in the nuclear navy including both ship development and personnel selection. Because of his contributions and knowledge, he was promoted to vice admiral and allowed to remain on active duty well past normal retirement age. He retired in 1982 after sixty-three years service and at the age of 82 and was promoted to full admiral at that time.

General Mathew B. Ridgway, U.S. Army (1895–1993)

Ridgway was commissioned a 2nd lieutenant in the infantry after graduating from West Point in 1917. He missed combat in World War I, assigned to the 3rd Infantry in the States. Between wars, he served in China, Nicaragua, and the Canal Zone in both command and staff positions. As war came again, he was assigned to the War Plans Division and promoted to colonel in 1941. Ridgway was promoted to brigadier general and became first assistant division commander, and then commander of the 82nd Airborne Division. He was promoted to major general and was in command in combat in Sicily and Salerno. He jumped with his division into France on D-day, and helped defeat the German Ardennes offensive as commander of the XVIII Corps. He was promoted to Lieutenant General in 1945. Ridgway took over command of the 8th Army in Korea, and when Truman fired MacArthur, Ridgway replaced him as UN Commander and Commander-in-Chief Far East. He succeeded Eisenhower as NATO Supreme Commander and was promoted to full general in 1952, and became Army Chief of Staff the following year. He retired in 1955, and was chief executive of several business firms prior to his death.

Field Marshal Erwin Rommel, German Army (1891–1944)

Erwin Rommel entered the German Army as an officer-aspirant at the age of 19. A year and a half later he was commissioned a second lieutenant. During World War I he served in France, Romania, and Italy, and was wounded twice. He received the Pour le Merite, then Germany's highest military decoration for his actions during the battle of Caporetto. After the war he held various infantry command and training assignments. Rommel published his book, *Infantry Attacks,* based on his World War I experiences in 1937. He was responsible for Hitler's personal security during the annexation of the Sudetenland, the occupation of Prague, and the Polish campaign. After commanding the 7th Infantry Division during the invasion of France in 1940, Rommel was given command of the Afrika Korps in Libya in 1941. His military skill earned him the name, "The Desert Fox." When the British surrendered to him at Tobruck, he was promoted to field marshal. After his defeat at El Alamein by Montgomery, he was given command of Army Group B in Northern Italy. Rommel also was in command when Army Group B opposed the allied landings in Normandy. He was wounded in an allied air attack in 1944. While recovering, he was implicated in the attempt to assassinate Hitler. He was given the choice of standing trial or committing suicide. Rommel chose the latter.

Field Marshal Maurice Comte de Saxe, **French Army (1696–1750)**

Maurice de Saxe was born in Saxony and joined a Saxon infantry regiment as an ensign before he was a teenager. By the age of 16, he was a cavalry colonel. His early combat experiences were as a member of German and Austrian forces, but after expending his wife's fortune, his father purchased a commission as a colonel for him in a German regiment in French service. In the later wars in which he participated, he was in French service, sometimes opposing his former allies. These included the War of Polish Succession (1733–38) and the War of Austrian Succession (1740–48). In 1736 he was promoted to lieutenant general, and later to Marshal of France. Given command of the Army at Flanders, de Saxe captured Brussels, Antwerp, and invaded Holland. His exploits earned him a promotion to a unique rank: Marshal-General. He retired soon afterward and fell dead of what his death certificate called "une surfeit des femmes."

Lieutenant General John M. Schofield, **U.S. Army (1831–1906)**

Schofield graduated from West Point with the class of 1853. At Wilson's Creek during the Civil War in 1861, he was a major of artillery. Although this was a Union defeat, Schofield won the Medal of Honor and was made a brevet brigadier general of volunteers. From 1861 to 1864, he commanded various departments in the west and commanded the XXIII Corps under Sherman during the Georgia campaign. After the war he was sent on a secret mission to Napoleon III to warn him off from his adventures in Mexico. He served as Secretary of War, as Superintendent of the U.S. Military Academy (West Point) and succeeded Sheridan as General in Chief of the Army.

General H. Norman Schwarzkopf, U.S. Army (b.1934)

"Stormin Norman" Schwarzkopf graduated from West Point in the class of 1956 and was commissioned in the infantry. He served two combat tours in Vietnam, first as an advisor to the Republic of Vietnam Airborne Division, and later as commander of the 1st Battalion, 6th Infantry, 23rd (Americal) Infantry Division. He was wounded and decorated for valor during both tours of duty. As a major general he was deputy commander of the Joint Task Force which carried out the Grenada invasion. When Iraq invaded Kuwait in 1990, he was a full general in command of U.S. Central Command. As such, he became Commander–in–Chief of all forces in Operations Desert Shield and Desert Storm. For the first time, he employed his air power in an independent role prior to launching his ground campaign. This plus his strategy resulted in a stunning success in destroying enemy forces and winning a great victory with minimum allied casualties. He received numerous awards and honors from U.S. and foreign governments. Schwarzkopf retired from the Army in 1991 and since then has been involved as an NBC consultant and commentator.

Lieutenant General Willard W. Scott, Jr., U.S. Army (b. 1926)

Willard Scott graduated from West Point in 1948 and was commissioned a second lieutenant in the field artillery. He commanded artillery units in Europe, Korea, and Vietnam. As a brigadier general, he commanded V Corps artillery in Europe, was named commander of the 25th Infantry Division in 1976, and as a lieutenant general returned to the V Corps as its commander. In 1981, Scott was named Superintendent of his alma mater, the United States Military Academy at West Point, a post he served in for five years until his retirement in 1986.

Colonel General Hans von Seekt, German Army (1866–1936)

Von Seekt served in senior positions in the German Army during World War I culminating in service as Chief of Staff of the Turkish Army. After Germany's defeat, he became head of the Reichswehr, and served from 1920–1926. He is credited with organizing it so that it could be readily expanded, which eventually occurred under Hitler. He was adviser to the Chinese Nationalist Army 1934–35, and wrote the book, *Thoughts of a Soldier* in 1930.

Major General Ariel Sharon, Army of Israel (b. 1928)

"Arik" Sharon joined the Haganah, the underground defense force allied with Israel's labor party, while still a teenager and during British occupation. At the outbreak of Israel's War of Independence in 1948, he was a platoon commander. He served in that capacity, as an intelligence officer, and as a company commander. After studying at Hebrew University, he was given command of Unit 101, responsible for retaliation for terrorist raids. At the time of the Sinai Campaign of 1956, he was in command of the 202nd Parachute Brigade which opened the campaign by dropping one battalion at the Mitla Pass in the Sinai desert. Before the Six-Day War of 1967, Sharon headed various assignments including Head of Training and became a brigadier general. During the Six-Day War, Sharon commanded one of three armored task forces which carried out Israel's offensive in the Sinai. He retired from active duty, but was recalled and led the armored division which crossed the Suez Canal cutting off Egyptian forces during the Yom Kippur War. He left the Israeli Army again as a major general and went into politics helping to form the Likud (conservative) party. He served in a number of posts, including Minister of Defense.

General Philip H. Sheridan, U.S. Army (1831–1888)

"Little Phil" Sheridan graduated from West Point in 1853 and was commissioned in the Infantry. Prior to the Civil War, he fought Indians in Texas and Oregon. As the war broke out in 1861, he was a 1st lieutenant. A year later he was a cavalry colonel winning his promotion to brigadier general. In 1863 he became a major general and corps commander in the Army of the Cumberland. When Grant was made General-in-Chief, he had Sheridan reassigned to the Army of the Potomac as commander of the Cavalry Corps. He defeated Confederate cavalry commander, Jeb Stuart and became commander of Union forces in the Shenandoah in 1864. In his absence, his army was surprised at Cedar Creek and was near defeat. But the mere presence of Sheridan was enough to turn the battle around. His riding to the battle was immortalized in poetry (Sheridan's Ride). After the war, he commanded several military divisions and departments and was commander of a number of campaigns against the Indians. This included Custer's defeat at the Little Big Horn in 1876. He was promoted to lieutenant general and eventually became General-in-Chief of the Army in 1883. He was promoted to full general after leaving the Army and just prior to his death.

General William T. Sherman, U.S. Army (1820–1891)

"Uncle Billy" Sherman graduated West Point in the class of 1840 and was commissioned a 2nd lieutenant of artillery. He saw his first action against the Seminole Indians and also saw service during the Mexican War. He resigned his commission in 1853 and started a building firm which failed. He then became a lawyer. In 1859, he became Superintendent of Alexandria Military Academy, which later became Louisiana State University. He was recommssioned as a colonel of infantry in 1861 and was a brigade commander at The First Battle of Bull Run. Sherman was promoted to brigadier general a month after the battle. He served under General Grant in the West, became a corps commander, and eventually succeeded Grant as commander of the Army of Tennessee and became a major general. In November of 1864, he began his "march to the sea," destroying everything in his path for sixty miles. After the war he was promoted to lieutenant general and became a full general and General in Chief in 1869, a post he held for fourteen years.

Marshal of the Royal Air Force Sir John Slessor, **Royal Air Force (1897–1979)**

Slessor joined the Royal Flying Corps and fought during World War I. He briefly left what had become the Royal Air Force (RAF) after the war, but gained a permanent commission in 1920. Slessor was promoted to Air Commodore just before WW II. He played important roles as commander of Coastal command, Chief of the RAF in the Mediterranean, and as a senior commander during the invasion of Europe. After the war he was promoted to Marshal of the RAF and became Chief of the Air Staff.

Field Marshal Sir William Slim, **British Army (1891–1970)**

Slim received military training through Britain's Officer Training Corps, and was commissioned a 2nd lieutenant just prior to World War I. During the war, he served in various combat assignments in the Middle East and in France. Between wars he served in the Indian Army and again in the Middle East. He was promoted to the rank of brigadier just prior to World War II. During the war, Slim held successively higher combat commands, and he captured Baghdad and invaded Iran. He was transferred to India, and fought the Japanese in

Burma, Malaysia, and Indonesia and throughout South East Asia. He was made Chief of the Imperial General Staff and promoted to field marshal after the war.

Major General Perry M. Smith, U.S. Air Force (b. 1934)

Smith was commissioned a 2nd lieutenant in the Air Force after graduating from West Point in 1956. He flew fighter aircraft for several years, and was then sent to Columbia University where he received a PhD in International Relations, before flying fighters in the Vietnam War. He returned to teach political science at the Air Force Academy from 1969 to 1970. After several other fighter assignments in both staff and command posts, he was promoted to brigadier general and became Air Force Director of Plans. As a major general, he was Commandant of National War College. He retired from the Air Force in 1986 and started his own company to teach and consult in leadership. During the Gulf War, he became an analyst and commentator for CNN. In 1998, he publicly resigned, despite threats of legal action, to protest the lack of investigation before CNN aired a television special based on slanted evidence which alleged that U.S. forces used poison gas against American defectors in Vietnam. The report was later proven false, and Smith was hired by NBC.

General Joseph Stilwell, U.S. Army (1883–1946)

"Vinegar Joe" Stilwell graduated from West Point in the class of 1904 and was commissioned in the infantry and sent to the Philippines, fighting against rebel forces. Afterwards, he served several tours of duty at West Point as a language instructor and, during World War I, served in France as a colonel and chief of intelligence of a corps. After the war, he reverted to the rank of major. Between wars, he served several tours of duty in China including as a battalion commander and later as military attaché. He was promoted to brigadier general in 1939, major general in 1940, and given command of the III Corps and promoted to lieutenant general in 1941. Shortly thereafter Stilwell was named commanding general of the U.S. forces in the China-Burma-India Theater. He trained and equipped three Chinese divisions to U.S. standards. Stilwell was promoted to full general in 1944, but disagreements with Chiang Kai-shek led to his being relieved. He was made commander of Army Ground Forces, and later took command of the 10th Army on Okinawa. After World War II Stilwell was given command of the Sixth Army and the Western Defense Command. He died of stomach and liver cancer while on active duty.

Vice Admiral James B. Stockdale, U.S. Navy (b. 1923)

James B. Stockdale graduated from the Naval Academy in 1946 and became a naval aviator. Shot down over North Vietnam and imprisoned during his second tour of combat, he endured seven and a half years of torture and unsuccessful attempts to break him, including four years of solitary confinement. After his release, he became the symbol of moral and physical courage under adversity and resistance to ill treatment while a prisoner. He was awarded the Congressional Medal of Honor. After a senior flying command, he became president of the Naval War College, and on his retirement, president of the Citadel and later a Research Fellow at the Hoover Institute.

Major General J.E.B. Stuart, Confederate States Army (1833–1864)

James Ewell Brown "Jeb" Stuart graduated from West Point in the class of 1854 and was commissioned in the dragoons. He served in combat against the Indians in Texas and in Kansas in the cavalry. He was aide-de-camp to then-Lt. Col. Robert E. Lee and played a major role in the capture of Harper's Ferry from John Brown. He was promoted to captain, but resigned his commission shortly thereafter when Virginia joined the Confederacy. After distinguishing himself at the Battle of Bull Run, he was promoted to brigadier general, and soon became the preeminent cavalry commander serving Robert E. Lee's Army of Northern Virginia. His exploits included riding around the entire Union Army. He was criticized for failing to keep Lee informed of Union Army movement at Gettysburg and received a mortal wound almost a year later while opposing George Armstrong Custer serving under Sheridan at Yellow Tavern.

Sun Tzu, Ancient Chinese General (c. 500 B.C.)

Sun Tzu lived in the state of Ch'i which is part of modern Shandong and was a general in his monarch's army. He is best known for his book, *The Art of War*, which is not only the earliest known book on strategy and military theory, but has served as a handbook of Chinese warfare into modern times and helped to inspire Mao Tse-tung's work On *Protracted Guerilla Warfare*. Beginning with a translation by Lionel Giles in 1910, there have been numerous others into English, and today his ideas are also taught in most western military academies.

Field Marshal Prince Aleksandr V. Suvorov, Russian Army (1729–1800)

Suvorov served first as an enlisted man and was a sergeant by the time of the Seven Years War of 1756–63. His performance was so outstanding that he was commissioned and was soon a colonel. He fought in the Polish Civil War in 1768 and was promoted to major general. He fought in several wars in the late eighteenth century including one against the Turks. His performance against the French in Northern Italy as commander of Russian and Austrian forces in 1799 is considered masterful. He was age 70 at the time. However, a defeat, through little fault of his own, caused him to undertake a difficult, but successful and hazardous retreat during the Swiss campaign the same year. Czar Paul relieved him of command and stripped him of his titles. Ill, he died in disgrace the following year.

T'ai Kung Chiang Shang, Ancient Chinese General

Chiang Shang is one of the most mysterious of all those senior military officers quoted in this book. "T'ai Kung" is an honorific title. It was given to a man that did not achieve the rank of general until he was elderly, some say at the age of ninety. In his early life, Chiang Shang had an undistinguished career. Yet the T'ai Kung has been honored throughout Chinese history as the first famous general and strategic thinker. He came to prominence when he met the monarch King Wen. Wen had been alerted that a Sage would come to advise him in military matters and assist in his rebellion against the Shang dynasty. So when T'ai Kung appeared on the scene, King Wen soon recognized him as the Sage and made him Commander-in-Chief of his army. In this position for King Wen, and his successor King Wu, T'ai Kung triumphed over their enemies. His thoughts, *The Six Secret Teachings on the Way of Strategy*, is organized as a dialogue between T'ai Kung and his monarch.

Vice Admiral Joseph K. Taussig, U.S. Navy (1877-1947)

Taussig graduated from the United States Naval Academy in 1899 and during World War I was commander of the destroyers USS Wadsworth and USS Little. A year and a half before the Japanese attack on Pearl Harbor on December 7, 1941, he warned a Senate Committee of an eventual war with Japan. His warning stirred up a hornet's nest in Washington and the Navy Department repudiated his "poor judgment" for his testimony. Three months before Pearl Harbor he was retired with the rank of Rear Admiral. Although at mandatory retirement age, this was viewed as a reprimand for his statements to the Senate. Two years later, he was recalled to service and eventually was promoted to vice admiral.

General Maxwell D. Taylor, U.S. Army (1901–1987)

Maxwell Taylor graduated from West Point in the class of 1922. He was commissioned in the corps of engineers, but transferred to the field artillery four years later. His assignments before World War II included France, Japan, and China, and he soon became known within the Army as a linguist. Shortly after the war began he was promoted to colonel and became chief of staff of the 82nd Airborne Division. As a brigadier general he helped plan the airborne landing in the Sicily campaign and later went behind the lines in a dangerous mission to determine the feasibility of an airborne drop on Rome. He commanded the 101st airborne Division and parachuted in the Normandy invasion. In 1945, he became Superintendent of the United States Military Academy and later commanded the 8th Army late in the Korean War. He was promoted to full general as commander of all U.S. Army forces in the Far East, and afterwards Army Chief of Staff. Taylor retired in 1959, and wrote a book, *The Uncertain Trumpet,* which attacked the U.S. doctrine of massive retaliation. President Kennedy recalled him to active duty and he became Chairman of the Joint Chiefs of Staff. Later, he was appointed ambassador to South Vietnam.

Marshal of France Vicomte de Turenne, French Army (1611–1675)

Born to a dukedom, de Turenne entered his uncle's army as a private at the age of 14. He distinguished himself in battle and was appointed a captain. At the age of 29, he entered French service and was given command of a regiment. His performance in many battles during the Thirty Years War won him additional promotions and he was made Marshal of

France and sent to rebuild the German Army after a disastrous defeat, which he did, winning many victories. In 1672, he successfully led the French Army on the left bank of the Rhine in the War of Triple Alliance. He was killed in action three years later, mourned by his troops as a great leader and by colleagues as an accomplished strategist and tactician.

General George Washington (1732–1799)

At the age of twenty, Washington was appointed adjutant for southern Virginia and was commissioned as a major in the militia. He served in combat during the French and Indian War as a major in the British Army, and his success led to his promotion to colonel. He was with British General Braddock during his disastrous defeat at the Battle of Monongahela in 1755, and was given credit for helping the survivors to withdraw successfully. He was promoted to brigadier general as a brevet (honorary rank) prior to his leaving the British Army. The Continental Congress appointed him general to command the rebel army as America's War for Independence broke out ten years later. During the war he faced the Herculean task of building an army and fighting the British at the same time. He had neither trained soldiers nor trained commanders. Eventually, with French help, he was able to force Lord Cornwallis to surrender at Yorktown, Virginia in 1781, thus bringing an end to the war. He was elected first President of the United States in 1789 and reelected in 1792, but refused a third term. He was briefly recalled to active duty during a crisis with France in 1798.

Field Marshal Archibald P. Wavell (1883–1950)

Following family tradition, Wavell was commissioned into the famous Black Watch regiment. He fought in South Africa in the second Boer War of 1899–1902, served in India, fought in France during the early part of World War I, but then was sent to the Middle East and served on General Allenby's staff. By 1939, he was a general himself and was posted to command British forces in the Middle East. Despite totally inadequate forces, he was sometimes surprisingly successful, as when he conquered Italian East Africa and invaded and defeated pro-Axis governments in Iraq and Syria. However, his offensive against Rommel failed, and Churchill replaced him. After commanding for a brief time in India, he was again sent out with minimum resources to hold the line against the Japanese. Although defeated, his service was apparently recognized because he was promoted to Field Marshal and made Viceroy of India. He retired in 1947.

Field Marshal Arthur Wellesley, The Duke of Wellington (1769–1852)

"The Iron Duke" was educated at Eton and commissioned an ensign at the age of 18. He became a lieutenant colonel by purchasing his rank (a custom in the British Army at the time) and led his regiment successfully in battle in the Netherlands. Sent to India, he distinguished himself. He was made a governor and successfully led British forces in a campaign against native forces, which made his reputation, and enabled his promotion to brigadier general. He commanded British armies in Denmark, Portugal, and Spain. Eventually he was named Commander-in-Chief of Allied Forces in Northern Spain and in 1813, field marshal. On Napoleon's return from exile, Wellington commanded the Anglo-Dutch army. With his Prussians, he defeated Napoleon at Waterloo. Wellington was made Commander-in-Chief on the death of the Duke of York, and served in other posts including that of Prime Minister.

Admiral Elmo R. Zumwalt, Jr., U.S. Navy (1920–2000)

Elmo Zumwalt graduated from the United States Naval Academy in 1942, commissioned an ensign, and was assigned to destroyers. He saw action in the Pacific at the battle of Leyte Gulf. After the war, he held a number of destroyer commands and other posts on larger ships, including serving on the U.S.S. Wisconsin in combat during the Korean War. He commanded the U.S.S. Dewey, the first guided missile ship and was promoted to the rank of captain. In 1965, he was promoted to rear admiral and commanded Cruiser-Destroyer Flotilla 7. From 1966–68 he was commander of U.S. Naval Forces, Vietnam as a vice admiral and became a full admiral and Chief of Naval Operations in 1970.

Marshal of the Soviet Union Georgi K. Zhukov, Soviet Army (1896–1974)

Zhukov was conscripted into the Imperial Russian Army at the age of 19. He served in various cavalry units and became an NCO during World War I, winning two Orders of St. George. In 1918, he joined the Red Army and commanded a cavalry squadron during the Russian Civil War. Afterwards, he attended several war colleges, including the Kriegsakademie in Germany and the Frunze Military Academy in the Soviet Union. In 1939 he commanded the Soviet First Army Group which defeated the Japanese Sixth Army. He held important commands after the German invasion of 1941, including command of the Western Front during the German attempt to take Moscow. His forces captured Berlin, and he was the Soviet representative accepting the German surrender. After the war, he held a number of region commands until becoming Deputy Minister of Defense in 1953, and Minister of Defense two years later. He was dismissed from this post by Khrushev in 1957.

INDEX

227